Reading Y
Child's Hand

Reading Your Child's Hand

Anne Hassett

CARROLL & BROWN PUBLISHERS LIMITED

First published in 2006 in the United Kingdom by

Carroll & Brown Publishers Limited
20 Lonsdale Road
London NW6 6RD

Design Laura de Grasse
Special photography Jules Selmes
Photographer's assistant David Yems
Image manipulation Michael Wheeler

A CIP catalogue record for this book is available from the British Library.

ISBN 1-904760-35-X

10987654321

Reproduced by Colourscan, Singapore
Printed and bound in Italy by MS Printing

Contents

Foreword

This book offers insight and information to parents regarding the innate character of their offspring. Palmistry is not just a parlour game or a bit of fun consigned to a carnival or funfair but a skill and an art, which has been around for thousands of years and has stood the test of time.

Armed with the knowledge contained in this book, you will be able to assess your child's character, skills, talents and abilities. Once aware of your child's strengths and weaknesses, you should be able to help him or her capitalize on strengths and talents and minimize the effects of the less fortunate aspects of character.

Many adults, caught up in the wrong careers, fervently wish that someone had been able to guide them when they were younger. Having spent years (and money) training for something, being educated for careers that, later on, they absolutely hate, they feel guilty about all the resources invested and stay on in jobs they loathe. Since all of us spend a great part of our lives at work, if we are not enjoying what we are doing, how can we be successful or happy? No wonder we develop "dis-ease"!

You can help your child to avoid this life-damaging pitfall and find a career that will bring happiness and fulfilment and, consequently, success. Someone once said that the secret to success in life is to do what makes your heart sing.

The science of palm reading is an exact one and it takes years of practice to be able to accurately interpret the information revealed by the hand. This book has a specific and definite aim – that is to help parents to unlock the secrets of their children's hands; therefore. I have kept it as simple and uncomplicated as possible.

Introduction

Wouldn't it be wonderful if you could find a way to help your child to develop his or her potential in life?

How great it would be to be able to help your son discover his gifts and talents and develop and use them. And through acknowledging his shortcomings, be able to work with them or even in some cases to be able to eliminate them.

Wouldn't it be wonderful to help your little girl to find her abilities and skills and to find a way to overcome weaknesses and help her to reach her full potential?

There is a way.

By understanding what is "written" on your child's palm, you can identify and nurture his talents; you can anticipate and help to control antisocial characteristics, and you can encourage leadership qualities and appreciate your child's quickness to learn or be patient with his tendency to procrastinate.

With the information in this book, you will be able to decipher the lines, read the lumps and bumps and interpret the shapes of fingers and general characteristics shown by the shape and size of your child's hand.

The information provided will help you to guide your child towards studying subjects in which she will excel, and ultimately to the right career. You can ensure your child does not waste years of precious time studying a subject that she is not "cut out for" and ultimately may not enjoy or be successful at. Far better to be able to guide your child towards a fulfilling and lucrative career! All this can be read in your child's hands.

So what is in your child's hand?

I'm sure that like almost every parent that ever was, when your little miracle was born, you could not help gazing fondly at him for hours on end. You probably examined every feature and looked at every little tiny detail, like his perfectly formed little eyelashes and the beauty of her little pink mouth. You may have held his feet in your hands and gazed in wonder at the sheer perfection of those little tiny feet and the delicacy of his little toenails. You probably tried to uncurl her tightly clenched little fists and stared at the palms of her beautiful little hands, wondering what all those little lines on the palms actually meant. Every newborn exemplifies the miracle of creation.

Nature makes no mistakes. There is not a thing in the human body that is not there for a reason

Sceptics will argue that the lines on the hands are nothing more than flexure lines; if this were so, then surely wouldn't all hands be the same?

The lines on the hands are not something that develop as we use our hands; they actually appear very early on in fetal development. The Life line begins to show as early as the eighth week in the development of the fetal hand and the Head and Heart lines appear soon after, all three being evident by the third month.

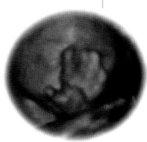

At 23 weeks old, this fetus has clear lines on his hand.

At birth, your little baby has the lines clearly marked and they will show his entire potential. Your newborn has her CV in her hand!

I refer to the lines on the hand as "nature's barcode" and in some parts of the world, palm reading is used as part of the recruitment process. I have long said that it would be wonderful if palm reading could be used in schools, particularly at the time when subjects are being chosen, so that a child could be guided towards the most suitable path for her future happiness and success. What a lot of heartache and wasted time that would save her and her parents!

Many enlightened parents bring their children to see me and I will read their hands only for career guidance; I do not focus at this age on what the child's romantic or marital prospects might be. They will have to address those issues soon enough.

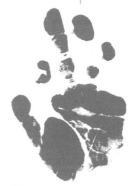

This one-month-old child's print shows his major lines clearly.

At the critical stage when your child has to refine her studies, based on her academic strengths and character, the lines on the hands should be studied so she can be pointed in the direction of the most appropriate career choice, the one that will make the most of her abilities and will pave the way towards success. Your child can be steered away from subjects that are going to be a struggle and which will only cause her anguish and frustration later on. Rarely can someone be successful at something she does not enjoy. Your child's heart will not be in it.

A little history

Chiromancy (from the Greek word *Xier* or *Chier* for hand) or palmistry as it more commonly known, dates back to very ancient times. Thousands of years ago, people in ancient Egypt or Chaldea, as well as in China and India, used palmistry as a predictive tool. In fact, documents have been discovered in China that date back to at least 5,000 years that chronicle the study of the human hand. I have great respect for Chinese palmistry and have incorporated some aspects of it in this book. There is also reference to hand reading in the Indian Vedic texts from 2,000 BC. Palmistry is still a much respected profession in India, with knowledge being passed from generation to generation. Japan is also a very rich source for this ancient science.

Hippocrates (460-357 BC), the father of modern medicine, used the study of the hands as a diagnostic tool and clinical aid.

The great Aristotle (381-322 BC) is reputed to have been fascinated by the hands. He was tutor to Alexander the Great and it is said that Aristotle wrote a treatise on the human hand for him. Alexander was a keen student of palmistry and was such an ardent admirer of the science that it was he who had the knowledge translated into Latin, thus making palmistry available to scholars throughout Europe.

Emperor Caesar was also a student of palmistry, and when a prince presented himself at the royal court, Caesar asked to see his visitor's hand. After inspecting it he boldly denounced him as an imposter, no doubt throwing the court into chaos but, in the end, Caesar's amateur palm-reading ability proved to be quite accurate.

There are many references to the human hand and its significance in the Bible. One specific reference to palmistry is in Job:37 where he says, "He sealeth up the hand of every man, so that all men may know His work." There is another mention of hands in Proverbs, which talks about "length of days in her right, and riches in her left".

About the middle of the 16th century, the Christian church began a vigorous crusade against all written knowledge in book or manuscript form, which contained any reference to hidden or occult knowledge. The Church was jealous of any knowledge that it did not author and therefore could not control. In 315 AD, a papal edict condemned palmistry as a pagan practice and anyone found engaging in this art would be immediately excommunicated from the church ... or worse! This drove palmistry underground in Europe for nearly 1,000 years. It was during the Renaissance that notable scholars as Paracelsus (1493-1541) and Robert Fludd (1574-1637) reintroduced palmistry as a subject worth study and respectability.

In the Muslim faith, the hand also has religious significance. It is seen as a sign of protection and if you are travelling in Islamic countries, you will see little plastic models of hands hanging from the sun visors of buses and cars. In Islam, the five fingers of the hand represent the different members of the Holy Family. The thumb represents Mohammed and the index finger the Lady Fatima. The middle finger represents Lady Fatima's husband Ali, and the remaining fingers symbolize their sons, Hassan and Hussein. The five fingers also represent the five principal commandments of the Muslim faith.

In the Hindu and Buddhist religions, palm reading is taken much more seriously than in the Western world, but then they have a long and honourable history of hand analysis.

Apart from such worthy persons as Paracelsus and Fludd there were many more eminent scientists and physicians who made a study of the hand. In the last century, Julius Speer wrote a book entitled *The Hands of Children* to which the eminent psychologist Carl Jung wrote an introduction, saying "Hands, whose shape and functioning are so intimately connected with the psyche, might provide revealing, and therefore interpretable, expressions of psychological peculiarity, that is, of human character." The Austrian doctor, Charlotte Wolff, did a great deal to further the cause of hand analysis.

Fables and myths were created for each symbol engraved in the human hand to make them easier to memorize. In Western palmistry, the parts of the hand were named after Roman gods and goddesses, not necessarily for superstitious reasons, but as an aid to memory and an association with the qualities of the particular gods and goddesses for whom the part of the hand was named. In other parts of the world, the parts of the hands were named differently, but meant the same thing. If you have even a little knowledge of astrology, you will find it immensely helpful in understanding the nature of the gods and goddesses mentioned. Bear in mind that these gods and goddesses represent archetypes common to our Western civilization

Today, the importance of palm reading is gaining renewed interest in the corporate world as an alternative to personality profiling. With standard personality profiling, answers can be cunningly given to offer a different profile than the real one; the hand, however, will always give the true personality and a skilled hand reader will be able to interpret this with accuracy. The study of someone's handwriting has long been acceptable in the business world as a tool for character analysis, but now the study of the hand itself, or palmistry, is fast becoming popular.

Palm reading for parents

With even a basic knowledge of palm reading you will be able to guide your child to the full expression of the innate abilities he was born with, thus ensuring fulfilment, joy and happiness in your child's life. You also can see if there are any blockages, weaknesses or challenges that your child can be helped to overcome. As the song says,

"Accentuate the positive, eliminate the negative."

When we have a clearer understanding about our faults and failings, as well as our gifts and talents, we are in a stronger position to allow ourselves to grow. Sometimes our challenges are our greatest growth opportunity. If we had no challenges we would grow very little. I saw a sentence in a book recently that said, "If you want to know where your next area of growth is, go towards your greatest fear!"

You cannot cushion your child from life's lessons, but you will be able to help her respond to challenges armed with certain skills and strengths. By gaining knowledge of these skills and strengths through examining her handprint, you will be able to guide your child forward. You will also be able to help her to overcome any weaknesses and help eliminate any character defects.

When looking at the hand, there are many elements that collectively make up a palm reading, most of which are covered in this book. All aspects need to be taken into consideration and only by combining them will you achieve a full understanding of your child.

Remember, your child is born with the lines on his or her hand. These lines are indicators of character and personality, of disposition and temperament, so your newborn's hand can be deciphered and an idea of any strengths and weaknesses determined from day one.

There are two ways in which you can read your child's hand. The first one is by taking a handprint of your child's hand (see instructions on how to do this on page 78). The advantage of this method is that you will have a copy of your child's handprint to keep and refer to as she grows. You will then be able to assess her progress and help her develop her talents. Handprints do not always show all of the lines clearly, so I suggest that you make notes to keep for future reference, or you could make a tape recording of your observations.

The second method of reading your child's hand is by taking the dominant hand in yours and actually looking at it. This is my preferred method as, with it, you can get a feel of the flexibility, texture, temperature and colour – and none of the mess that making a handprint entails! Again, I would suggest that you make a recording of what you see to keep and refer to as your child grows and develops.

A serious palmist will thoroughly examine both hands and will look for dormant talents that may be lurking or unacknowledged in the "unconscious" (normally left) hand.

So how do you go about it?

It would be best to have your child sitting beside you rather than facing you as then you will not be looking at the hand upside down. In this way, you can compare the marks on your child's hands with the illustrations in this book.

First determine the general attributes of the hand.	Test the rigidity or flexibility of the hand; feel the temperature and look at the colour. (pages 18–19)
Then observe the shape of the hand.	Which category of hand-shape does your child's hand fit in to. (page 21)
Next, look at the length of the fingers in relation to the palm.	Keeping the illustrations of finger lengths and shapes in front of you, observe and record those of your child. When looking at fingers, remember to observe the nail shapes, too (page 48). Without him expecting you to do so, press your fingers against your child's thumb and feel how he resists the pressure. How does he hold his thumb in relation to his hand? How long or short is the thumb? Has it got a "waistline" etc? (page 37)
Next, take a look at the mounts.	Compare them to the illustrations (page 50) and note how well formed they are.
Then look at the lines.	I would start by looking at the Life line, then the Head line followed by the Heart line, as these are the major lines of the hand. Then you could look at the Fate, Apollo, Mercury and Health lines. (pages 57–70)
And, lastly, seek out the unusual marks and signs.	Stars, crosses, squares, etc., may be present (page 71). One sign in a hand may contradict another, but then we are all a mass of contradictions. It's very rare indeed to find a hand that fits a pure hand type, although it can happen.

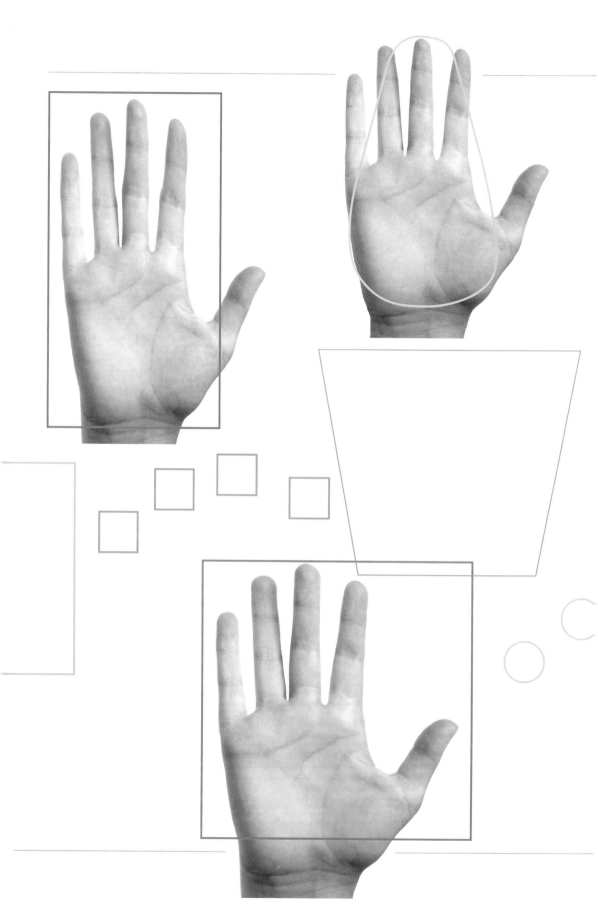

The whole hand

Hands come in different sizes, textures, colours and shapes and each characteristic can tell you a great deal about your child. While it is very rare to find a hand that fits a pure hand type, it does happen. Try to determine the shape that most resembles that of your child's hand, and work from there.

Handedness and size

In order to give a complete reading of palms, both hands are looked at and compared, but you would only do a complete reading and analysis of your child's dominant hand. Dormant talents, however, may be lurking or unacknowledged in the "unconscious" hand, so a more serious palmist would always examine both hands.

Righty or lefty?

About nine out of every 10 children over the age of five use their right hands to write and throw. Left handedness affects only about eight percent of the population. A small number of children can use either hand for all activities (when they are known as ambidextrous) whereas some use one hand for certain activities and the other hand for others. A child who has a left-handed parent has an increased likelihood of being left handed but she is still more likely to be right handed. If both parents are left-handed the chance of being left-handed is increased further. It has not yet been established whether genes determine handedness or whether it is factors, as yet unidentified. Interestingly, identical twins do not necessarily have the same hand preference, which supports the theory that handedness is not just due to genes.

If your child is right-handed, the left hand reveals what she was born with – her inherited tendencies or her unconscious drives.

A right-handed child

Your child's RIGHT hand depicts what she will consciously make of her life; what strengths and abilities she will work with throughout her life and how she will develop.

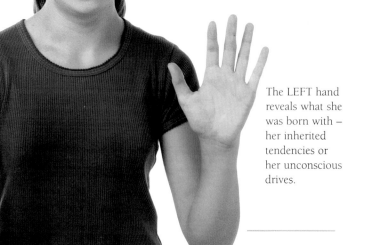

The LEFT hand reveals what she was born with – her inherited tendencies or her unconscious drives.

Left-handed children

If your child is LEFT-HANDED, this is the hand that represents your child's conscious mind and how that conscious mind will influence her future. This child's RIGHT hand is the unconscious one and will hold the inherited tendencies. About eight percent of the population is left-handed and there is a higher incidence in male children. In the past, many left-handed children were forced to write with their right hands. This practice can have very powerful, far-reaching and sometimes damaging psychological effects, and happily, it is now falling into decline.

Your child's right hand depicts what she will consciously make of her life; what strengths and abilities she will work with throughout her life and how she will develop. It makes sense when you think about it: you are conscious and aware of the things your right hand is doing, like waving, pointing, brushing your teeth, opening a door etc., whereas with your left hand, half the time, you have little idea of what it is doing. You would miss it if it was unable to perform, but we do rather take our passive hand for granted.

If your child is left-handed, then the functions of the two hands, as far as palm reading is concerned, are reversed (see box, above).

Referring to a right-handed person, the gypsies used to say, "your left is what you're born with, your right is what you make of it". You also could say the left is the potential and the right is how that potential is actualized. A client of mine recently commented, "I thought your left hand was your inner self and your right hand was your outer self." She was right, it's just another way of putting it!

Size matters

The first thing to do when looking at your child's hand is to establish the size of the hand, which should be in proportion to the size of the body. The size of the hand tells you a huge amount about that individual (see overleaf).

Check for size

If your child's hand is SMALL in proportion to the size of his body it indicates an ability to engage on a large scale. "Small hands do large work." Small-handed people see the big picture well and can envision things on a grand scale. They can sort out bigger things but can't be concerned with the finer detail; they need someone else to do that. Small hands think big and they're good at being in charge. They make good overseers, managers or managing directors or will very often have their own business. They do slip up on attention to detail and will need the help of others who will attend to that for them. Their hand-writing is often large and expansive.

If your child's hand is LARGE in proportion to body size, it indicates an ability to do intricate work well. "Large hands do small work." It seems a contradiction when we say that large hands are good at working with minute detail as we wonder how such "clumsy" looking hands can make fine and intricate movements. Large-handed children can be seen working with mosaics or fiddly bits while ignoring what's going on around them. They can focus on the littlest things, like staring into the microscope to study bacteria. They also are deft with their fingers; they make good surgeons, watchmakers or will be good at doing the finest engraving or embroidery. Large-handed children will not, however, see the big picture very clearly. They are not afraid to "think big", but thinking big is just not part of their natures. But, like everything else, if you have a child with a proportionally larger hand, you can encourage him or her to be aware of this characteristic and maybe do something about it. The handwriting of a large handed person will, as a rule, be fine and small.

Texture and flexibility

A palm that is elastic but fairly firm to the touch denotes a healthy constitution and a positive and buoyant outlook on life. A short, flabby hand denotes a love of luxury and an inclination to laziness. In the latter, there may be a strong underlying sensuality. A child with this type of hand will need a mixture of discipline and encouragement.

A "wooden" palm – one that is dry and possesses little elasticity – denotes a child with a nervous nature who is prone to worry. He or she will need a lot of reassurance and positive input.

The flexibility of the palm reflects the flexibility of the character. A too stiff palm indicates rigidity in the make-up and, at the other extreme, a palm that is too flexible will denote someone who can be pushed around.

Colour and temperature

White or pale hands show lack of vitality and a tendency to see the negative side of things.

Hands with a bluish colour may have circulatory problems. Possessors of such hands will tire easily and may be lacking in vigour. A visit to your health practitioner would be a very good idea in this case.

Red hands have an abundance of energy and this needs to be channelled. If this energy is not directed into something positive, like sport, it may turn into frustration and consequent aggression. This child needs to be kept busy and active or she may become a little trouble-maker.

Adverse indications may be overcome by such methods as acupuncture, where the energy or chi is encouraged to flow harmoniously as it should.

Hands that are cold at room temperature show a child who lacks generosity and may have a tendency towards selfishness and self seeking; the old adage "Cold hands, warm heart," does not seem to be validated by palmistry! This child needs to be encouraged to think of others.

The child with a hot hand will be full of enthusiasm and will need constant activity to avoid being bored. A child with a hot hand could go on to achieve a great deal in life if that enthusiasm is channelled positively.

negative

white may mean negativity

unhealthy

blue could indicate health problems

energy

red might denote energy

Narrow or broad palm

If your child's palm is narrow (longer than wide), it indicates a tendency to be self-centered. Your child will need to be encouraged to think of others and it will help him greatly to show him that selfishness will only make him unpopular with his peers. Self-centeredness is sometimes a result of your child's sensitivity. This child will have a good attention to detail and will be very conscientious. It also means that he has a strong ability to concentrate which, when well directed, can prove fruitful. There is a need to encourage this child not to give himself a bad time when he does not reach perfection.

HANDS-ON PARENTS
Working on the premise that the first seven years of a child's life are the formative ones, this is the time when the work can be done to help your child to overcome his or her defects and strengthen any positive characteristics.

I always remember a Chinese lady saying to me years ago, "We should not strive to be perfect, as there are no perfect people. We should strive to be excellent!" I have never forgotten that, as it left me off the hook! My own desire towards perfection had driven me to giving myself a hard time about many things. Perfection is unattainable by humans. Excellence is much more within our grasp. The Persians used to say, "Nothing but Allah is perfect", which is why they always put a deliberate flaw in their carpets. We all have deliberate flaws. Being too hard on ourselves is not constructive.

If your child has a broader palm, her hand seems open and large. Broad palms symbolize a broad and positive outlook on life and an innate sympathy and generosity. Children with broad hands are naturally kind and affectionate. They can be considerate and, due to their generous natures, will be sociable and get on well with people. However, they dislike isolation and especially dislike working on their own. As part of a team, however, these children thrive, particularly in outdoor activities. As they are sympathetic and generous, as adults, they will do well in careers where caring and organization is needed, such as in the hospitality trade, public relations or the caring professions.

The child with a broad palm tends to be affectionate and sociable.

MAIN HAND SHAPES

There are many different shapes of hands and in this book I will concentrate on the five main ones. Although the shape of your child's hand may change as he or she grows, lines and mounts will nearly always remain the same as they appeared on the day your child was born. New lines appear if new dimensions are added to the psyche, as when your child learns a new skill, develops a latent talent or gains new insights – but, generally we are who we are.

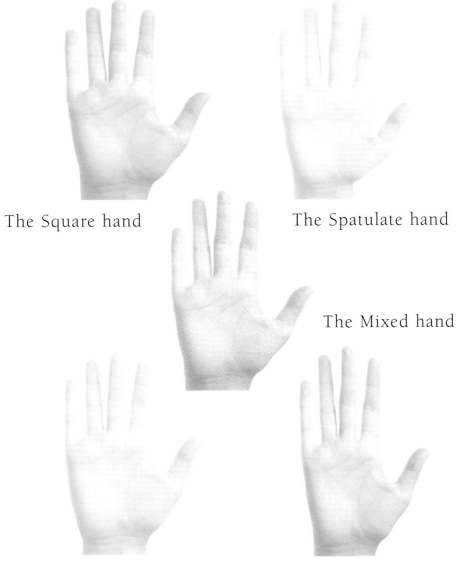

The Square hand   The Spatulate hand

The Mixed hand

The Psychic/Sensitive hand   The Philosopher's hand

the SQUARE hand

engineer

BUREAUCRAT

ACCOUNTANT

Distinctly square in appearance, this hand looks square at the wrist and again at the base of the fingers; the tips of the fingers also will be square.

We have an unflattering expression in our language where we may refer to someone as being "square", meaning that the individual is considered more boring than others. In fact, this is most unjust. We need "square" people in our lives as they are very competent organizers. They like to know where things are and where they stand in relation to others. They are steady and reliable and usually can be counted on in any situation. They are unlikely to be impulsive or slapdash.

Square-handed children are practical and level headed. Their views are often conventional and they have a great respect for law and order. They are emotionally stable and generally dependable. The negative side of this personality is that these children can be very obstinate and often refuse to see another person's point of view.

If your child has a square hand, he will be an organizer and planner and like things in "boxes". He will like to categorize things and for things to be "right" – a place for everything and everything in its place. Your child also will like to categorize people, and will be easily fazed if someone around him gets "out of his or her box" because your child will like to maintain the status quo.

Full of common sense, square-handed children rarely give in to emotional outbursts; in fact, they find it difficult to understand emotional people. They hate confusion, resist change and can be lacking in adaptability, especially if they have rigid thumbs. They like method, structure and rules and regulations. If your child is square-handed you will find him generally reliable and obedient. He will like order, however, so it would be good to encourage him to be a bit more adaptable.

Square-handed adults make excellent engineers, librarians, analysts, police officers, town planners, accountants and bureaucrats – in fact, any type of work that requires thoroughness and a systematic approach. They also make good civil servants or members of the armed forces.

the tips of
the fingers
will also be
square

TOWN PLANNER

police officer

ANALYST

librarian

square at the base
of the fingers

distinctly
square in
appearance

square at
the wrist

Adventurous children

Sometimes there is a pronounced curve to the percussion side of a square hand. The percussion side of the hand is the side opposite the thumb. If the curve between the Mercury finger and the wrist on the percussion side of the hand is low down nearer to the mount of Luna, the child who possesses such a curve will have a huge reserve of physical energy combined with fortitude and persistence. When there are other signs in the hand (such as a Head line, which slopes to the mount of Luna), children having these hands will be adventurous and will love physical adventure. It is said that Scott of the Antarctic had just such a formation but I have not been able to verify this.

Mercury
finger

percussion
side

Head line

mount
of Luna

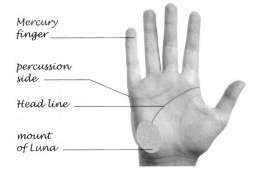

the SPATULATE or artisan hand

builder

SCULPTOR

COOK

craftsperson

EXPLORER

The shape of this hand is marked by the fanning out of the fingertips to form a spatula shape. The palm, instead of being square, is broader where it joins the fingers. The tops of the fingers, too, are often spatulate or spoon shaped. Thinking of how we use spoons, for getting into things, the same applies to a spatulate hand. Spatulate-handed children have a great love of action. They are very independent, dynamic, energetic and confident. Practical in day-to-day aspects, they are "hands-on" people.

If your child has these hands, she will love to get in touch with the world and will get many of her impressions through her sense of touch. Spatulate-handed children are full of drive and ambition and enjoy activities on a material plane, where they can actually touch, feel and sense through their hands. They can sometimes be unconventional and love to have daring and original plans and ideas. They like to break the rules and are usually found at the cutting edge of new inventions or ideas.

If the spatulate hand is soft and flabby, this child will have these qualities in a dormant rather than an active state. She will have the ideas but not the determination to carry them out. Support and encouragement, at an early age, can make all the difference for this child.

These hands are also sometimes called "Artisan's" hands; the owners of such hands are very creative.

Creative children

Occasionally, a child with a spatulate hand also may have a well-developed Jupiter finger, a high mount of Jupiter or a strong Apollo line. These reinforce the notion of creativity. If a child has all three, he'll be a real star.

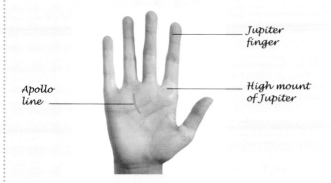

Apollo
line

Jupiter
finger

High mount
of Jupiter

Spatulate-handed adults make good builders, sculptors, cooks, craftspeople, explorers, chefs, gardeners, interior designers, carpenters and entrepreneurs.

fingers fan out
to form a
spatulate shape

spoon or
spatulate tops
of fingers

palm is broader
where it joins
the fingers

CHEF

gardener

interior designer

carpenter

ENTREPRENEUR

the PHILOSOPHER'S hand

judge

SCIENTIST

TEACHER

priest

This hand is usually very long in proportion to the size of the child and the difference between this hand and others, is that the knuckles are quite pronounced. It's as if the thought processes stop at each of the knuckles of the hand because these children think long and hard about things. That which is their greatest strength is also their greatest weakness. They are the thinkers and seldom do anything spontaneously; they give a lot of thought to everything they do. Such thought can be a great thing when matters are of great importance as they won't be rash or hasty, but the negative side is that these children find it difficult to make quick decisions, which may lead to them being indecisive and they will procrastinate.

Much depends on the work these hands do; they would be very suitable for deep and detailed work such as research. Children with these hands are good at figuring out crosswords, conundrums and the "meaning of life" but because they prevaricate and procrastinate, they can be very frustrating. If you are eating out with someone with a Philosopher's hand, for example, you can look at the menu and make a quick decision to have the chicken but 20 minutes or half an hour later, the person with the Philosopher's hand will still be undecided!

Children with Philosopher's hands live in the world of ideology and theory rather than the practical. This child will be thoughtful but hesitant and needs to be understood and guided into a career where this deep thinking and thoughtfulness will not be a hindrance.

This child will always have an innate sense of right and wrong and a deep sense of justice. He is conscientious and dignified and dislikes grossness and vulgarity of any kind. He has a tendency to be a fatalist and, very often, will have a strong Fate line (see page 69).

This child can sometimes appear withdrawn and may not easily make friends. If he is given understanding, he can be encouraged to open up a bit more. Where he does make friends, he'll make deep and lasting connections and be very loyal.

Children with these hands are seldom drawn to seek fame, and if fame does come, they take little pride in it.

Critical children

A child with a Philosopher's hand who also has a waisted thumb, i.e. the sides of his thumb curve inward slightly, may be overly critical and too much of a perfectionist. He needs to be encouraged to take a more relaxed attitude towards life.

Adults with Philosopher's hands would be effective in careers that require deep and philosophical reflection. They might be drawn to religion, philosophy, political science or law. They make excellent judges, scientists, teachers, priests, lawyers, detectives and researchers.

pronounced knuckles

hand is long in proportion to child's body

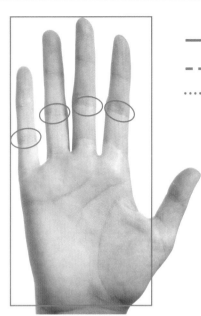

LAWYER

detective

RESEARCHER

the PSYCHIC/SENSITIVE hand

writer

ACTOR

HEALER

counsellor

VISIONARY

As the name suggests, the Psychic/Sensitive hand is the most sensitive of all the personality types. If your child has this type of hand, its shape will be conic – the end nearer the fingers will be narrow and that towards the wrist, broad.

This hand is commonly delicate in texture. Very often the mounts (see page 50) are quite soft. The whole hand has a seeming gentleness and sensitivity about it. The skin is usually delicate, too, and would remind one of the phrase "thin-skinned". It appears as if there isn't quite enough skin to keep the harsh world out.

Children with these hands are extremely sensitive and pick up on atmospheres and moods around them. They can walk into a room and gauge the emotional temperature of what is going on in that space. Obviously, they would be wonderful in any kind of job that requires this kind of sensitivity, such as becoming a psychic consultant, or performing counselling or healing. They are often people who have a great appreciation of the natural world and its beauty and are sometimes extremely aware of nature spirits. They enjoy peaceful and tranquil environments. They usually make good gardeners being so "at one" with the rhythms and cycles of the natural world. The trouble they have with gardening, however, is that although things do grow well for them, they aren't always robust enough to do the hard work.

As I mentioned earlier, it is very unusual to find a hand that falls purely into a particular type; there is always a bit of a mixture. But if your child's hand falls into the shape described as the

Adults with a Psychic/Sensitive hand will prefer careers such as writer, actor, healer, counsellor, visionary, mystic, priest, set designer, movie maker and philanthropist.

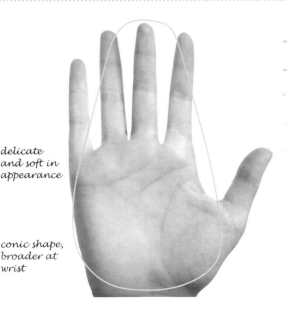

delicate and soft in appearance

conic shape, broader at wrist

MYSTIC

priest

SET DESIGNER

movie maker

philanthropist

Psychic/Sensitive, she will be extremely vulnerable. A child with this type of hand falls in love easily as she will be a very romantic individual and have idealistic notions of love and relationships. She could live in "cloud cuckoo land". The child with a Psychic/Sensitive hand is sometimes quite impractical and can be a bit of a pushover and gullible with anyone with a hard-luck story.

Your child will be very caring and won't like to be scolded or told off, so if you have to discipline her, you must do so in a caring and subtle way. You will find it much easier to lead your child than to drive her.

If you are the parent of a child with a Psychic/Sensitive hand, you will need a lot of patience, tolerance and understanding when dealing with her because she can be quite fanciful and sensitive and needs much care and attention. Dealing with peers is quite difficult for her. Listen carefully to her as your actions will affect her. If she's tearful and sad, she needs a good "listening to" and a big hug and she'll be fine. She is quite resilient and will recover quickly and, as she is very much in touch with the unseen world, she will have a lot of help from the unseen beings.

You may find your child has an imaginary playmate who is very important to her. If this is the case, you should never ridicule your child for having one or belittle the imagined "friend". Just because you don't see it, it doesn't mean that your child does not! The world we live in is full of wonder and we lose so much as we grow older and more cynical. The world, seen through the eyes of the Psychic/Sensitive child can be a truly magical place.

the MIXED hand

gambler

ENTREPRENEUR

property speculator

The mixed hand is the most commonly seen hand. It may show two or more aspects of the previous hand types. The shape of the palm might be square but the fingers might be conic. In fact, this hand may show several finger types. Therefore one must always take all the aspects of the hand into consideration.

The child with the mixed hand will have many and varied interests. He will, generally, be capable of multi-tasking and will do many things at the same time. He will get along well with nearly everybody and will have something in common with most people. This child loves variety and is quick to adapt. He will be quick to master the basics of most tasks. The danger is that he becomes "Jack of all trades and master of none". There is a certain merit in the latter, however. If he's a master of a certain trade and there is no work in his line, he is in trouble. The "Jack or Jill of all trades", on the other hand, can quickly turn around and adapt to something entirely different, so is seldom out of work for very long.

On this hand, the Apollo and Fate lines (see pages 68 and 69) are often clearly shown and these people are often great believers in luck and destiny. They often become gamblers and gamble with life and money, especially if the Apollo (or ring) finger is longer than the Jupiter (or first) finger.

We usually interpret the word "gambler" as something negative, but the gamblers of the world are those who get an idea and take a chance on it. They are the entrepreneurs and the innovators. They are also the property speculators and the venture capitalists.

As this hand is mixed, the owner is very versatile and can often turn his hand to anything. Other factors in the hand, therefore, must be taken into consideration to determine the best future possibilities.

Successful children

If a child with a mixed hand also has both a clear Fate line and a well-defined Apollo line, he'll do very well in life and will be successful at everything he turns his hand to.

Mixed-handed adults make excellent entrepreneurs and business people. They are not afraid to take a chance and invariably become successful.

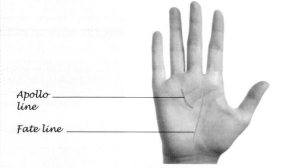

Apollo line

Fate line

*mixture of
different
aspects of
various
hands*

Never judge by just one
aspect of the hand

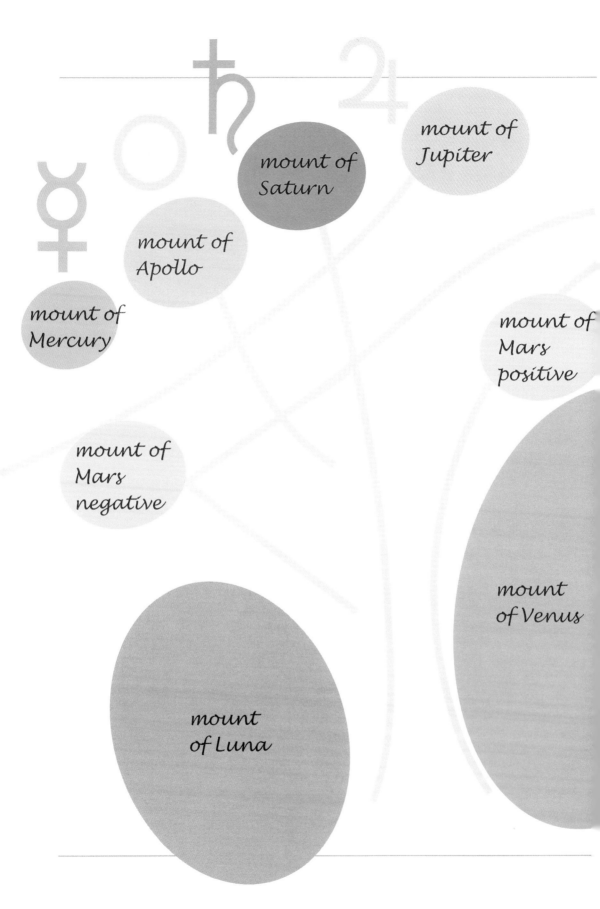

The fingers
and thumbs

The fingers are one of the most critical factors when deciphering a hand and all its wonders. A finger's length, shape, size and plumpness all indicate specific things. The thumb is not generally depicted as a finger and is dealt with separately.

In Western palmistry, each finger is named for a Roman god, and is associated with the qualities of that celestial being. While those of you with a knowledge of astrology will easily recognize the energies that each of these gods represents, for those unfamiliar with astrology, I've included some useful information about the traits under each finger.

Finger tips
The tips of your child's fingers and thumb have shapes that must be examined in a palmistry reading. Spatulate (spoon-like), conic or square, the tips can give some extra clues as to whether the child is tactile or may even have healing abilities.

Fingers
The length, shape, angle of opening and appearance of the phalanges all provide different information about your child's various spheres of interest.

Phalanges
These are the sections of the fingers and each finger has three phalanges – the bottom, middle and nail phalange. Each one of these, like the entire finger, gives vital clues to your child's nature.

Thumb
This is the only digit of the hand which, for some reason now lost in the mists of time, is not named after a Roman god.

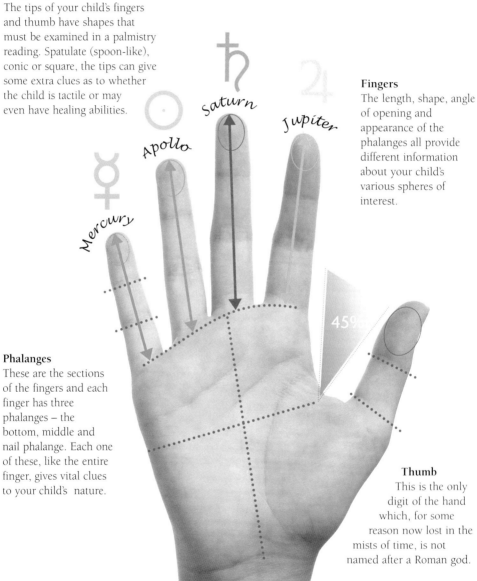

Mercury
Apollo
Saturn
Jupiter
45°

Thumb

The human thumb is very unique. It is entirely different to the thumbs of primates as only humans have opposing thumbs. Unlike primates, humans can touch the tips of their thumbs with the tips of their index fingers. This quality of the thumb gives it the ability to grip and use tools. From that ability has developed the power to reason and use logic. The use of tools has been of supreme importance in the creation and development of our entire civilization.

When babies are first born, they generally hold their thumbs in their palms and cover it by their fingers. If the thumb remains in this position for some while after the birth, there is often concern regarding the mental strength or delicacy of the child. Ideally, the thumb will emerge in the first seven days. If you ever have occasion to observe someone who has had a severe mental shock or a breakdown, you will notice that the thumb retreats into the hand, as in the newborn. When the thumb begins to emerge again, it is a sign that the person is on the mend.

The thumb relates to the will and reason. Will and reason are also unique human characteristics. A good strong thumb indicates a good strong will. The length of the thumb is also of significance here. If it is longer than average (see right), it indicates a child with a powerful will; if it is shorter than the average length, it indicates a child with a lack of determination.

Flexibility of the thumb is another important aspect when reading palms. If the thumb yields easily to the pressure I put on it, this often indicates the child is a bit of a pushover – not able to stand up for himself. When it resists the pressure, there is a sense of tenacity or stubbornness (we call it tenacity when it's perceived as a good thing and stubbornness when it's not!) but there is strength, and this child won't be told what to do easily.

If the thumb is very large and it resists strongly, the child can be a bully, hence the expression "under the thumb". A bulbous tip makes bullying tendencies even more likely (see page 37). Negative qualities can, however, be turned around and redirected.

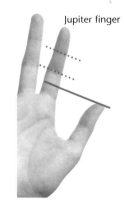

Jupiter finger

The top of the average thumb comes half way up the first phalange (or joint) of the Jupiter or index finger

Before the general populace could read and write, the signature to important documents was made with the thumbprint.

The Phalanges

The thumb has two phalanges (unlike the fingers, which have three). The formation of these phalanges and what they mean are important to understanding your child. They should be roughly the same length. The bottom phalange, the one nearest the

When I read a child's hand I usually press his thumb to detect resistance. I will do this without telling the child beforehand as, if he is forewarned, it takes the surprise element away and he will be prepared.

The angle of the thumb

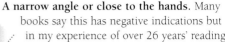

The normal angle is around 45 degrees. A child who has this angle will have a good capacity for adhering to normal standards of life, such as a sense of fair play and a good, practical common-sense outlook.

A narrow angle or close to the hands. Many books say this has negative indications but in my experience of over 26 years' reading hands, my interpretation is that when someone holds his thumb close to his hand it indicates a "closed" or nervous person who doesn't have much will. He may have been bullied or may not have had the opportunity to express himself to his full capacity. A child with this trait may have overbearing parents or there may be some other oppressive adult in his life such as a teacher, relative or nanny. When the influence of the overbearing person or bully is removed, the thumb will generally return to the "normal" position. This indicates a return of confidence in the child.

Some palmists have interpreted this positioning of the thumb as indicating a child with selfish tendencies. I feel it quite likely that someone who lacks self confidence will, indeed, think of himself. This can be corrected. As the child is taught to gain respect for himself and as he begins to love and like himself, he will have more to give to others and will be more inclined to reach out to interact with those around him.

45°

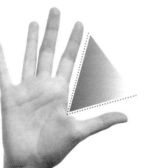

Held at an angle greater than 45 degrees away from the hand, it indicates someone with true characteristics of individuality and a very strong personality. This child will need careful guidance and handling if she is to remain balanced and not become overbearing.

HANDS-ON PARENTS

If the thumb forms a right angle to the rest of the hand, which is very rare, it indicates someone who is a leader of people, is innovative and will make her mark on the world; a real "mover and shaker". Obviously, a child with this formation will need very careful guidance indeed. She should be encouraged to find a role model to emulate. It would be good to provide her with books or videos on such renowned world figures as Mahatma Gandhi, Martin Luther King, Mother Teresa, Anne Frank, Nelson Mandela or some other selfless world personage who has been an inspiration to the masses.

hand, may have a little "waistline" to it and, if this is distinct, it is often "owned" by a child who is self-critical and self-analytical. She demands perfection from everyone else around her but also expects perfection from herself. If you're aware of these tendencies, you can work to transform them. The lines don't change very much but the shape of the hand can change, sometimes quite dramatically, as the character changes.

It is important to study the top of the thumb. If it is cone shaped, it indicates a child who is impulsive and who doesn't reason things well. If it is pointed, it shows a child who needs constant reassurance and confidence boosting; leadership isn't for him but he can be a loyal follower. This child can be indecisive but is good at routine work and is generally quite reliable.

When the top of the thumb phalange is square, it indicates a very strong personality. If your child has such a thumb, she is capable of decisive action and combined with other strong signs in the hand, these are leadership qualities. The child with this shape of thumb will have the qualities of persistence and dogged determination.

If the top phalange is bulbous, this child can be someone who doesn't reason things out and can be difficult and will lose his temper and resort to bullying. Ruled by passion, he will use his will to demand control. Little boys with this formation will more easily resort to fisticuffs than reasoning to get their own way. If you see this formation on your child's hand, he will need to be taught discipline and consideration for others.

Sometimes, this bulbous formation can be acquired through the habit of thumb-sucking. This habit often develops through feelings of insecurity but, like many childhood habits, can go on into adulthood if not discouraged.

On a long well-shaped thumb, if there is a swelling on either side of the nail, it indicates someone who is very independent and would do well being self employed.

If your child's thumb demonstrates negative aspects, with your guidance, they can be managed. Through hand reading, you have an opportunity to assist and educate your child at an early stage in overcoming traits that may work against his success.

"Waisted"

perfectionist

Cone-shaped

impetuous

Square-shaped

leader

Bulbous

passionate

So-called "double jointed" thumbs are not something to boast about. The owners of such a formation give in too easily, sometimes they "just can't be bothered".

Fingers

The fingers indicate your child's different spheres of interest. Each will be discussed below. However, you first might like to consider what the spacing of the fingers and their length might mean.

Spacing

Ask your child to hold her hand out in a natural relaxed fashion, palm up, and then observe how the fingers are held in relation to one another. If the fingers are splayed out, it indicates someone who is gregarious and extrovert. She will have confidence and mix well with others. If her fingers are extremely splayed out, she may be a bit of a performer or a show-off.

If she holds her fingers all scrunched tightly together, it shows that she is not sure of herself.

While her hands are held out, if the Jupiter (index) finger is held apart from the others, it shows a child who is very independent and is likely to have good leadership qualities; she is likely to be ambitious.

Hands can change. Some years ago, a client came in for a consultation. His Jupiter finger was rather short in proportion to the others. He admitted to a serious lack of confidence in himself. He hated his job, but did not have the belief in himself to make a change. We had a long discussion about his hopes and dreams and as a result, he decided to take the bull by the horns and do something he enjoyed much more. I saw him some time after and was amazed to see that his Jupiter finger seemed to have grown. Of course, fingers in adults don't grow, but what had happened was that with his newfound confidence, he was holding his hand and fingers quite differently and now his Jupiter finger looked as long as his Apollo finger.

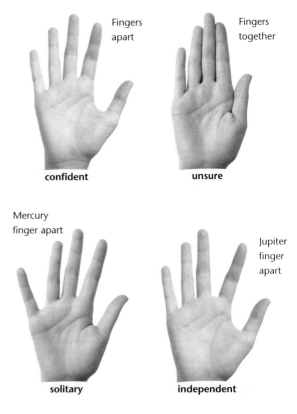

Fingers apart

confident

Fingers together

unsure

Mercury finger apart

solitary

Jupiter finger apart

independent

If it is the Mercury (little) finger that is held apart, your little girl will like her own space and will often prefer her own company. She will need time away from the crowd.

Length

The length of your child's fingers compared to that of his palm is a very important factor when reading the hand.

The way to measure the fingers is to first measure the palm (the length from the base of the wrist to the base of the middle finger). Then measure from the base of the middle finger right to its tip.

When a child's fingers are longer than his palm, it indicates a child who is very reflective and analytical, has attention to detail and is over-critical. This child is over-cautious and indulges in undue deliberation before taking any action. He procrastinates and prevaricates. If he makes a mistake, he will crucify himself over it and go to great lengths to ensure the mistake isn't repeated, which can be frustrating as it prolongs whatever he does.

Long-fingered children make wonderful researchers or accountants as they do what they do to the best of their abilities and work to exacting detail. They don't make quick decisions, however, and can be annoying as they can change their minds several times.

If your child's fingers are much shorter than the length of her palm, it indicates an impulsive personality. Impulsiveness, at its best, can be interpreted as enthusiasm and can give a certain sense of urgency to get on with things. It can even be interpreted as spontaneity! Such children are often good communicators; they get on with their work and are quick to learn. They have a mercurial quality and they are much happier leaving the "nitty gritty" to long-fingered people, as they want to get on and do things.

If the Mercury finger is well aspected (see page 46), this child can be good in media work of all kinds. She'll also make a good sales woman.

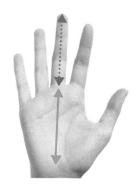

The "normal" length of the middle finger should be about $\frac{7}{8}$ths the length of the palm

HANDS-ON PARENTS
There are many methods available today for teaching and developing self worth. One method, which I know works, is to record a cassette tape for your child. Use your voice to tell your child how wonderful and special she is. Play it for her as she drops off to sleep, when her mind is in the alpha state. It works wonders. Your child's subconscious will take this on board, particularly as it is your voice – the voice she has been familiar with since she was in the womb.

the JUPITER finger ...

First/index finger

... stands for leadership.

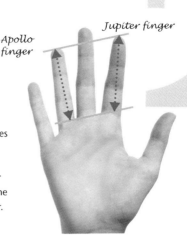

Apollo finger

Jupiter finger

Normal length
In the "normal" hand, the Jupiter finger will be the same length as the Apollo (ring) finger and reaches the base of the nail of the Saturn (middle) finger when the hand is open, palm up. Ideally, the Jupiter finger should reach half way up the nail phalange of the middle finger.

Jupiter in Roman mythology was the head or chief of all the gods. This finger could be said to be our chief finger. It is the finger with which we point to and prod things. It's the finger of leadership. It leads the hand.

The length and setting of the finger in the hand can tell you a lot about your child's leadership qualities and ability to assert himself.

When the Jupiter finger is longer and broader than the Apollo finger, by however small a margin, it indicates someone who naturally gravitates towards positions of authority, even if it is only to become head boy or sports captain. If it is excessively long, there is a certain ruthlessness, and the owner can have a tendency to be a bully and will want to be in control at any price. You don't argue with someone who has an unduly long Jupiter finger; his word is law and he likes to be obeyed. Luckily, this type of Jupiter finger is very rare. If you do come across it in your child's hand, look for other modifying aspects in the palm (such as a short thumb or a narrow angle of the thumb to the hand).

    If you find a long Jupiter finger in a Psychic/Sensitive child's hand, she is more likely to be a child who wants to control the nature of the environment around her. This is borne out of fear rather than strength.

If your child's Jupiter finger is shorter than her ring finger, it shows a child who is lacking in self-worth, someone who can have an inferiority complex. This can be worked on in your child if you recognize it. There are many methods available today for teaching and developing self-worth.

Although someone with a short Jupiter finger will be a follower not a leader, it is important that we have more followers than leaders in the world. Not everyone can be a leader, nor could an organization or an army function with all officers and no men! Being a leader is not an easy destiny; it leaves one wide open to all sorts of attack.

The Jupiter finger should be nice and straight in your child's hand and should "stand proud". If it leans towards the second finger, it indicates a child with a preoccupation with her home. These children often grow up to be Earth mothers, matriarchs, housewives and organizers. They like to rule the roost.

The Jupiter finger very rarely leans outwards, but sometimes a child may hold this finger apart from the others, which shows an extremely independent streak. This is the finger of uniqueness and individuality and, if it is naturally held away from the others, it indicates someone who likes to be a little bit different and who doesn't have a herd mentality. In children, this often shows itself as a strong rebellious streak, and later in life, they may have a tendency towards eccentricity. They are happiest when not conforming and will usually stand out in a crowd. They like to be different and independent of the world.

Jupiter phalanges

The middle phalange has to do with the mental aspects of leadership and individuality.

The base phalange is concerned with the physical and material.

If it is fleshy and large this indicates someone who demands quality, seeks only the best and has a great sense of taste. These people make good chefs and tasters. If your child has a large, fleshy base phalange, she could be encouraged to go into the catering trade. She is also very hospitable. When older, she will love to give lavish dinner parties and insist on feeding people. Jupiter was also referred to as Jove – the derivation of the word jovial. The aforementioned formation on the hand indicates someone who is "the life and soul of the party".

When the middle phalange is long and strong it indicates a child with an aptitude for craftsmanship or DIY. These children love organizing and executing anything of a practical nature.

When a child has a shorter middle phalange it indicates a preference to delegate work; this child prefers to use his intelligence rather than physically involve himself in work. He likes to get others to do the donkey work for him. How very clever!

The nail phalange has to do with the spiritual ideals involved in leadership.

When the nail phalange is long and well developed, it indicates a child with an aptitude for spirituality. It indicates someone who likes to be in a leadership position but who has personal contact with others, such as an educator or counsellor. These children like to organize everything and to have direct contact with their work. This formation often can be seen on the hands of priests and other religious leaders.

the SATURN finger ...

Second/mediate finger

...stands for our background, career, property and responsibility. It is the finger of the controller and provider. This finger is more firmly attached to the wrist bone than the others so it is not as pliable.

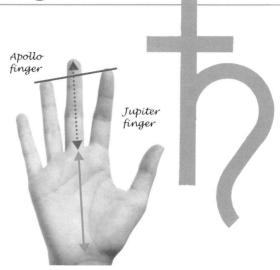

Apollo finger

Jupiter finger

Normal length
The average or normal length is about ⁷⁄₈ths the length of the palm and about half a phalange longer than the Jupiter (first) and Apollo (ring) fingers.

Saturn was the "great teacher". The influence of Saturn has to do with learning through life's practical lessons.

If the finger is longer in proportion to the other fingers, it indicates someone with an above-average sense of responsibility. Children with long Saturn fingers can become quite solitary, aloof and unsociable. Possessors of very long middle fingers will often deserve the label of someone with what is known as a "Saturnine disposition". Every effort must be made with a child like this, to jolly him out of it and to encourage him not be so serious.

Due to their aloofness and aloneness, children with long Saturn fingers don't mind spending time on their own. They have a great sense of dedication and enjoy solitude. This is the sort of personality that in later life would be quite happy being holed up in some forgotten far-flung outpost or working as a lighthouse keeper or independent researcher. As children, those with long Saturn fingers, will be content to spend long periods of time in their own company. Do bear in mind that if your child is such a one, he is not antisocial, he is just more

comfortable with his own company. He thinks a lot and has very definite ideas about many things. He will often come out with very profound statements and you will wonder where on earth he got his ideas. He may have a tendency to be hard on himself.

Children with long Saturn fingers are dedicated and quite studious. They are unlikely to get the sort of school report that says "could do better" or "could try harder". They do, however, need to be encouraged to develop some social skills and not to take life so seriously.

If your child's Saturn finger is short in relation to her other fingers, she may have tendencies towards becoming a bit of a "flibbertygibbet", flitting from one thing to another with no staying power. Short Saturn-fingered children have bohemian tendencies and will often gravitate to careers in the theatre, art or music, especially if they also have an Artisan's hand (see page 24).

Children with short Saturn fingers love parties. In fact their dispositions are the opposite of the saturnine ones of children with longer Saturn fingers, and they will need to be given some guidance with regard to having some sense of structure in their lives in order to get a hold on things and apply themselves.

Saturn phalanges

The base phalange is concerned with Mother Earth.

If it is long, the child has an earthiness about him, and would make a good gardener, farmer, agriculturist or geologist, or he may get involved in archaeology, mining, crystals, etc. He loves getting his hands into the earth.

The middle phalange has to do with growth in animals, minerals or vegetables.

When it is short, there will be little interest in those things.

When it is long and well developed, it indicates someone who would love to cook and grow his own vegetables or an individual who likes creating recipes.

When it is quite long, the child could make a good scientist. She'll have a tendency towards intellectualizing and could become an intellectual snob. She may develop an attitude of superiority when dealing with her less cerebral peers.

The nail phalange has to do with intelligence, science and ethics.

If the nail phalange is short in your child's hand, he will be less intellectually inclined.

the APOLLO finger ...

Third/ring finger

... is named for Apollo, who was the Roman god of art and beauty. It is also sometimes referred to as the Sun finger, as Apollo was also god of the sun.

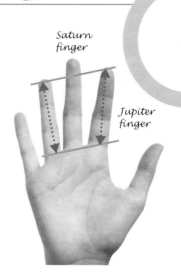

Saturn finger

Jupiter finger

Normal length
A well-formed Apollo (ring) finger usually comes halfway up the nail phalange of the Saturn finger and is considered "normal" when it is the same length as the Jupiter (index) finger.

If your child has a well-formed Apollo finger, this indicates someone with aesthetic tendencies. Your child will love beauty in his home. These children have the ability to make good designers; they will notice architecture, landscapes and clothes, and will be people who are born with the art of presenting food nicely. For them, everything has to look lovely. They have a widespread appreciation for beauty. They see it in many things and will create beauty wherever they go.

If an Apollo finger is as long as the Saturn finger, it indicates the finger of a gambler. Gambling, as we usually think of it, is not a very desirable activity and is not to be encouraged. The tendency to take a gamble, however, is not always negative, as it can indicate someone who will take risks in business or adventure. It could manifest in the individual becoming an explorer, entrepreneur or a stock market speculator. The owner of this formation will love the adrenaline flow that she gets from risk taking.

Tips of fingers

If your child has a spatulate tip on her Apollo finger, it really accentuates the quality of this finger and suggests someone who will be right at home with art and craftsmanship. She loves the idea of creativity and will make a fine actor, architect, designer or painter. She loves all forms of self-expression and may have a tendency to express flamboyance.

If your child's Apollo finger has a square tip, he has a good eye for proportion, design, form, size and shape. He would make a good architect, engineer or even wedding cake maker. He is less flamboyant than a child with a spatulate tip, and will be creative in a way where he "keeps his feet on the ground". His creations are usually of a more practical nature.

If your child has a conic tip on her Apollo finger it shows someone who is more in to appreciating the creations of others rather than actually creating something herself.

Apollo phalanges

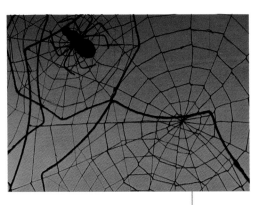

The middle phalange
has to do with the
appreciation of beauty.

When the middle phalange is long, your child sees beauty that
others may not notice – beauty in the simplest of things such as a
rainbow in an oil-slicked puddle or the intricacies of a spider's web.
Your child will find endless wonder in all sorts of things, which you
may not see. If you take note, you will have your own eyes opened
to the magic around you. It is not necessarily that your child has
the ability to create beauty but that she appreciates the beauty that
is all around her.

The nail phalange has to
do with the shape and
feel of beauty and
beautiful things.

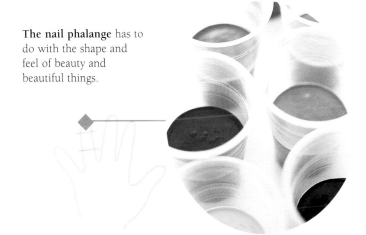

The base phalange is
concerned a love of
beauty and the ability
to create it.

If the base phalange is long and
well padded, it indicates a child
who likes comfort, especially in the
home. He is not usually the sort to
enjoy the deprivation of camping
and will complain loudly if he is at
boarding school and is deprived of
the luxuries he would enjoy at
home.

If your child's nail phalange is
long, it is the sign of someone
who has strong creative
tendencies. He has a
preoccupation with colour,
line, shape and form. He could
make a good architect, painter
or designer, and if there is a
"droplet" (see page 74) or
accentuated pad at the tip of
the finger, the owner will have
a keen sense of touch. He
loves to feel things – silk,
wood or pottery – and likes to
get his hands into things.
When fractious, he can be
soothed by stroking a cat or
cuddling a soft toy.

the MERCURY finger ...

Fourth/little finger

. . . stands for communication.

Assessing length
Measuring this finger is important. The finger is normally set low down on the palm and, due to the curve of the palm, it may appear that the finger is shorter than it really is. It must be measured from the base of the finger to the tip. Unless it is set unusually low in the palm, it will normally reach the base of the nail phalange of the Apollo (ring) finger.

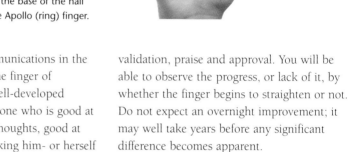

Apollo finger

Mercury is the god of communications in the Roman pantheon. This is the finger of communication. A good, well-developed Mercury finger shows someone who is good at communicating ideas and thoughts, good at talking the talk, good at talking him- or herself in *and* out of situations. We all know the expression "he can wrap you round his little finger". This is usually because such an individual has a well-developed mercurial quality in his personality.

If your child has a short Mercury finger, it indicates someone who finds it difficult to communicate or express ideas. She will need extra help to enable her to communicate and to express herself adequately.

Sometimes the Mercury finger is slightly crooked, and if this is not due to an injury (which may have happened at birth), it indicates a child with an inborn sense of low self-worth and he can have an unconscious desire to sabotage himself. By giving your child a better sense of how valuable he is, you can help him to overcome a great deal of this characteristic. This child needs constant

validation, praise and approval. You will be able to observe the progress, or lack of it, by whether the finger begins to straighten or not. Do not expect an overnight improvement; it may well take years before any significant difference becomes apparent.

If your child holds this finger close to the others on his hand, it indicates someone who likes to feel safe and secure. He won't like to stick his neck out and he likes being around other people. He feels safe in a crowd or as part of a community. He may become "clingy" and will need to be taught to open up to meeting and interacting with others.

If your child holds her Mercury finger away from her other fingers, it indicates a child who likes to have time to herself. She needs to get away from the crowd and to recharge her batteries. Even if she has good people skills, she will like to have her own space. For these children, having time to themselves is a necessity rather than a luxury and this desire will continue into adulthood. This desire for space needs to be honoured.

Mercury phalanges

The base phalange is concerned with the need for physical security.

A strong and well-developed base phalange indicates a child with an instinct to hoard, collect and gather things. If your child has this formation, you may well find that her room is quite cluttered and she can get very upset if you throw out old clothes, toys or any other of her possessions. She is good at holding on to her money. As long as there is not a tendency to miserliness, holding on to her money might not be a bad thing!

The middle phalange has to do with determination and good business skills.

The middle phalange on the Mercury finger is usually the shortest but if it is as long as the others, it indicates someone who has great tenacity; someone who won't give up easily and has a great sense of purpose.

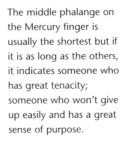

The nail phalange has to do with self expression.

The nail phalange, if long and well developed, indicates a child who is great at expressing himself in writing, public speaking or any form of self-expression. This will be given extra support if your child has the "writers fork" (see page 75) in his hand. This child will also have great powers of persuasion. A bulbous tip on your child's Mercury finger indicates someone who is bursting with ideas. He also is very humorous and has a gift for comedy.

When the nail phalange is short, your child will have difficulty in expressing herself no matter how intelligent she is. She will need extra help and encouragement. An extra-curricular class in public speaking or self expression would be invaluable to her.

Fingernails

It would be strange not to mention nails when I am discussing the fingers, particularly as the nails will give an indication of your child's health and vitality. Although the emphasis of this book is on character analysis and not health, it is worth mentioning health in passing, as the your child's health will greatly affect his ability to study, focus, communicate, concentrate and apply himself to his studies or career.

The horny part of the nail is the semi-transparent window through which you can see the state of the constitution beneath. Nails should be clear and their surface should be smooth. The colour of the nail should be pink. If the nails are a livid red, it can indicate a personality, which is "hot blooded" or quick tempered and therefore unsuited to a career requiring diplomacy, tact or consideration.

A pale nail indicates a child who hasn't got a lot of energy or vitality and this can be corrected, to a certain degree, through diet. A visit to a good nutritionist would be advisable. Acupuncture, to get the *chi* moving, also could be considered.

If there is a bluish tinge to the child's nail, it can indicate bad circulation or pulmonary difficulties. If you suspect your child is suffering from any form of disease, it is, of course, advisable to consult a doctor or a good complementary therapist.It takes six months for the nail to grow from the matrix to the tip of the finger. By observing the growth of the nail through the months, it is possible to look out for improvements, and you will be able to track whether therapy is having the desired effect.

Concave or "dish" nails often indicate a mineral imbalance and in this case it's worth observing the improvements on the nails after having given the child minerals. We often give our children vitamins and forget all about the important part that minerals play in nutrition and the body's health.

**concave
mineral
deficiency**

Convex nails are often referred to as "hour glass" nails, and can indicate lung problems; again consult a doctor.

When the nails are thin and flaky, brittle and inclined to break easily, there may be some dietary imbalance. White spots on the nails indicate a lack of calcium, sometimes lack of zinc.

Convex lines on the nails, which you can feel if you run your own nail across that of your child, can indicate a lack of iron. These lines will run from base to tip. An iron deficiency often leads to a child having a lack of energy, which will affect his or her ability to concentrate and to learn.

**convex
lung problems**

Concave lines, which usually run diagonally across the nail, will appear after a shock or trauma. They will also often appear after a general anaesthetic and you'll be able to watch them grow out.

HANDS-ON PARENTS

If your child develops signs of stress – shell-shaped nails, for example, he should be encouraged to engage in some activity where he can look after animals or be in touch with the earth. This will soon restore him to harmony.

large & square
slow to anger

long & narrow
gentle

Nail shapes

If your child has large square nails, he is even tempered and slow to anger. When he does get angry, it is often felt at the solar plexus level, and therefore he may suffer frequent stomach upsets. He will be inclined to internalize his anger rather than displaying it. Just as large square-nailed children are slow to anger, they can be equally slow to forgive. Small or tiny square nails usually belong to a child who easily becomes jealous. Such a child also can have difficulty showing his warmth or love.

If your child has narrow long nails, she usually exhibits a gentle temperament and prefers not to waste time being angry or upset.

Almond-shaped nails have been beloved of beauticians and artists for their aesthetic shape. The child with this type of nail will be inclined to show irritability rather than real anger.

almond-shaped
irritable

If your child has wide short nails, he has a tendency to be quick tempered; however, he rarely bears malice. His tantrums and outbursts are short-lived and soon forgotten – at least, by him.

Shell-shaped nails on a child's hand indicate someone with an ultra-sensitive nervous system. Sometimes the shell shape can develop on the hands of children who study too much or are overly conscientious.

wide & short
quick tempered

HANDS-ON PARENTS

Remember that any pattern in the hand is just ONE indication, and this may be tempered by other more fortunate indications found elsewhere in the hand.

shell-shaped
stressed

The "bumps" or raised pads of flesh on the hands are referred to as mounts. There are eight of them in total and they are named after the planets, which, in turn, were named after Roman gods and goddesses. The strength of any particular mount depends on its size when you compare it to the other mounts on the hand. In general those with more prominent mounts are more swayed by their feelings than are those with flatter palms and less-developed mounts.

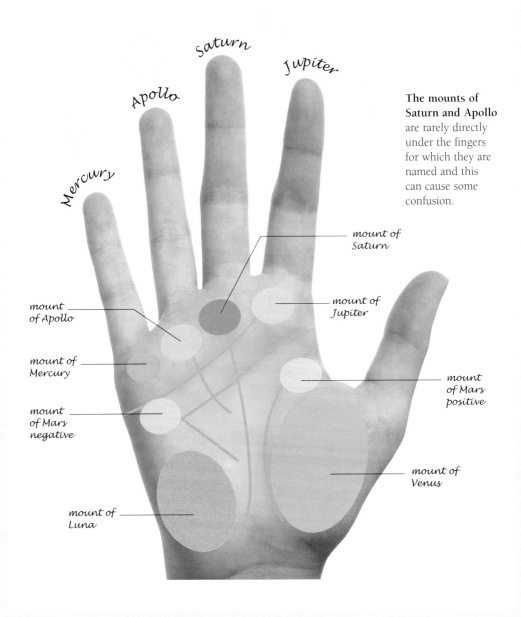

Saturn

Apollo

Jupiter

Mercury

The mounts of Saturn and Apollo are rarely directly under the fingers for which they are named and this can cause some confusion.

mount of Saturn

mount of Apollo

mount of Jupiter

mount of Mercury

mount of Mars positive

mount of Mars negative

mount of Venus

mount of Luna

Mounts

Mount of Venus

The largest mount of the hand is named after Venus, the Roman goddess of love. She is also the goddess of sensuality and the love of beautiful things.

The mount should not be too hard or too soft and should be comfortably firm and pink in colour.

This mount is to do with sensuality and sexuality. It denotes the appreciation of the senses and appetites for food and drink, aesthetic surroundings, home, comfort, art and the ability to enjoy physical passion. I sometimes compare children with high mounts of Venus to pussy cats. Cats like to be stroked, like nice food, always find the most comfortable place to lie down, seek out pleasure and comfort and don't like to be left out in the rain! That about sums up the characteristics of a high Venus mount!

A well-formed mount of Venus indicates a strong life force, high vitality, joie-de-vivre, energy and consequently a strong resistance to disease. When this mount is high and hard, it can indicate aggression, especially if it is red in colour. When the mount is flat, small and weak-looking, it indicates an absence of vital energy and physical passion and the person can often be lack lustre and lacking in passion for life.

The size of the mount of Venus is defined by the position of the Life line; the wider the sweep of the Life line into the hand, the larger the mount of Venus, which means a greater vitality and energy. When the Life line creates a narrow sweep, and consequently a smaller mount of Venus, there is little energy and appetite for life.

A too large or too soft mount indicates the sensualist; someone who may have a tendency to gluttony or an unhealthy pursuit of physical pleasure.

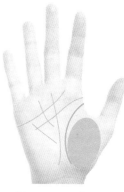

The mount of Venus is at the base of the thumb. It comprises the thumb ball and is outlined by the sweep of the Life line. This mount usually takes up about 25 percent of the palm.

Mount of Luna

The mount of Luna represents the connection with the unconscious mind and unseen worlds. Children possessing a large mount of Luna have vivid imaginations and are often quite creative. This mount is very connected to the back of the brain, where our imaginations reside. So if the mount of Luna is very well developed, more so than the other mounts, the child will have a very vivid imagination. If other characteristics in the hand are present, such as spatulate fingertips, he will make a good writer or painter, as he has to draw inspiration from his inner world. These children are very seldom lonely because when they are on their own they can retreat inwards and enjoy their fertile imaginations and rich inner landscapes. The negative side of this is they can have a tendency to daydream and withdraw. It is in

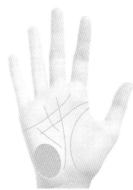

The mount of Luna is on the opposite side of the palm to the thumb (called the "percussion" side), just above the wrist.

day dreams that writers get their ideas, as do composers, painters, inventors and architects. If I was in charge of a school I would schedule at least a half hour of each day for day dreaming!

Psychic ability is a strong factor in the hands of a child with a high mount of Luna, as this is also the area that denotes intuition or wisdom from within (IN-tuition). Whether referred to as psychic ability, hunches or "gut feelings", it is a very useful ability to have. Most of the world's richest individuals have attributed their success to going with their hunches.

Children with a high mount of Luna will have a great appreciation of aesthetics in landscapes, design, architecture, art or music. This again depends on the other signs in the hand.

Children with well-developed mounts of Mars are active and energetic.

Mounts of Mars

There are two mounts of Mars on the hands: mount of Mars negative and mount of Mars positive. If both mounts are well developed, in relation to other mounts on the hand, the child will have a proactive personality, be a go-getter, sometimes with an element of anger. This child is impulsive and can rise to the bait easily. If the energy is directed constructively, perhaps he will be very successful at sports, achieving goals, etc. Again, this is where guidance from parent, guardian or teacher is invaluable.

Mount of Mars positive

This mount is an indicator of courage and decisiveness. If it is large in your little one's hand, it can indicate aggressiveness. This aggression, if directed positively, can give great determination to get things done. It will supplement other signs in the hand and add an extra dimension to leadership qualities.

A child with a too well-developed mount of Mars positive has a propensity to be tyrannical, especially if she has an overlarge thumb and a strong Jupiter finger.

Mount of Mars negative

This mount indicates courage that is more mental than physical. Children who possess this mount to any degree will have great moral courage. When it is especially developed, it will be quite difficult to place this child in a particular career, as she is so versatile and multifaceted.

The child with a well-developed mount of Mars negative has great staying power and will not easily yield to pressure. If this mount is flat in the child's hand, then combined with other less fortunate characteristics in the hand, such as an overlarge thumb, there can be defiance and obstinacy, even verging on cruelty. If your child has these formations, it is important that you are particularly careful during your child's formative years to help him develop more positive characteristics.

mount of Mars
negative _____

Mount of Jupiter

This lies squarely below the Jupiter finger. When it is high
and well developed, it augments the qualities of the Jupiter
finger, denoting good leadership qualities. The higher the mount, the more ambitious the individual. It is as if the mount gives energy to the qualities of the finger. This individual will have a great need to be in charge.

mount of Mars
positive _____

When the mount of Jupiter is absent or very flat, it decreases any ambition that may be shown by a well-developed or long Jupiter finger.

Mount of Mars positive is situated above the mount of Venus and enclosed by the Life line. The mount of Mars negative is situated between the Head and Heart lines and below the Mercury finger.

Mount of Saturn

This lies below the Saturn finger. If the mount of Saturn is high and well developed, it can indicate a sombre nature and an inclination to take life too seriously. There is often a sense of fatality, a belief that "what will be, will be". If the mount of Saturn is displaced towards the mount of Apollo, the child's more sombre characteristics will be softened. He will often develop a love of peaceful contemplation and meditation. A flat mount of Saturn denotes a person who does not take himself or life too seriously.

Mount of Apollo

This lies below the Apollo finger. If the Apollo mount is large, it indicates someone who loves to be centre stage. This child is someone with a large heart and generous disposition. She has a love of life and people, and loves to live life to the full. She can be full of "gusto". A flat mount of Apollo tones down this gusto quite a bit.

Mount of Mercury

This lies below the Mercury finger. If the mount of Mercury is well developed, it denotes someone with eloquence and plenty of ideas. This child will be quick witted and will sometimes possess the gift of oratory. A flat mount can indicate someone who may have lots of bright ideas but who has difficulty in expressing them.

A child with a flat mount of Mars negative and an over-large thumb can be defiant and obstinate.

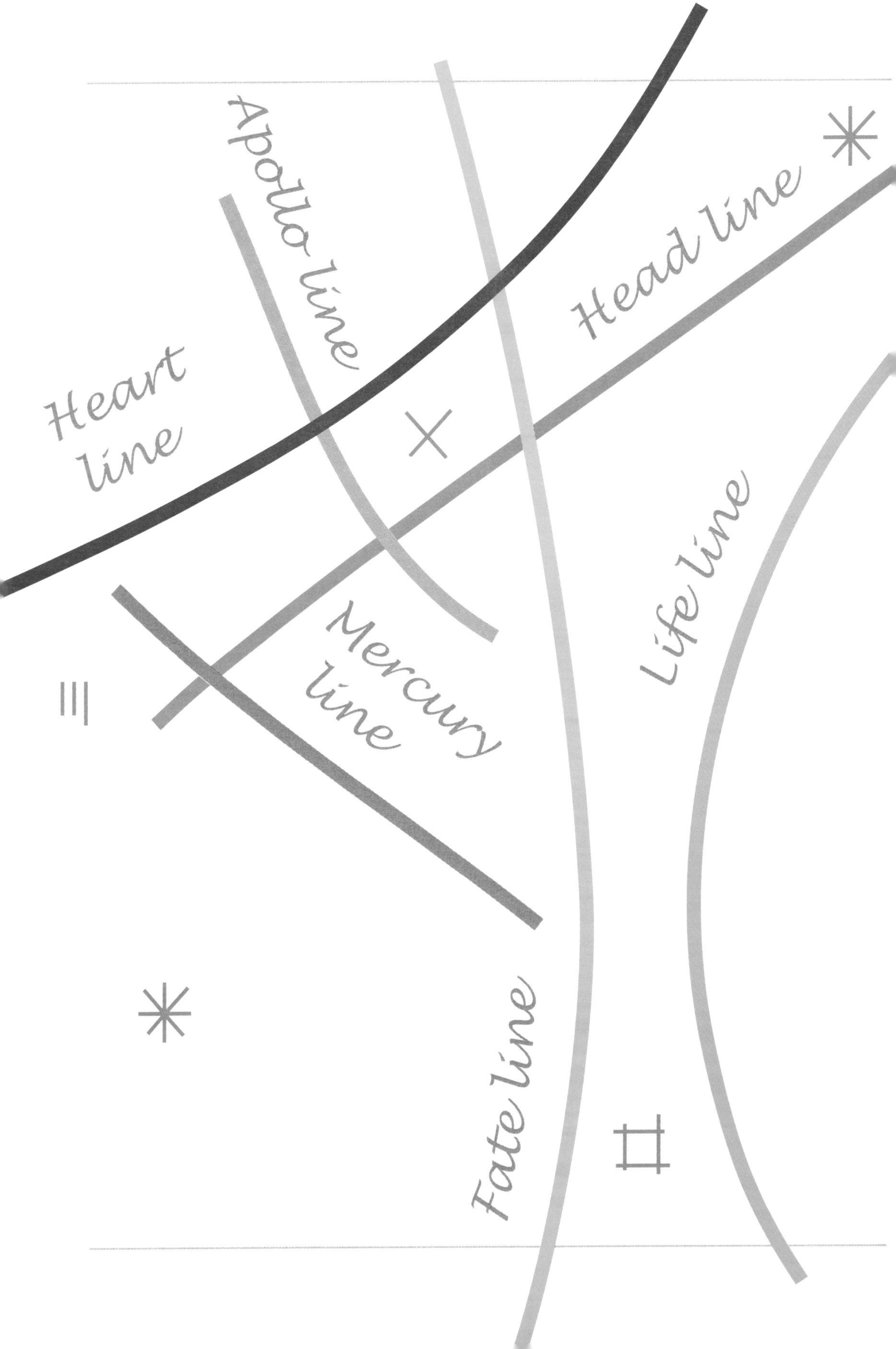
Apollo line
Head line
Heart line
Mercury line
Life line
Fate line

The lines and marks on the hand

Most people consider the lines on the hands to be the vital parts of hand analysis but, as you have gathered by reading all that has gone before, there is much more to reading palms than just looking at the lines alone. However, the lines are critical for an overall view of the personality.

There are six major lines: Life, Head, Heart, Apollo (or Sun), Fate and Mercury. Each major line has a set location and a normal position within the palm of the hand. When it is considered normal, it starts in a specific area and progresses along a certain course and terminates in a particular place.

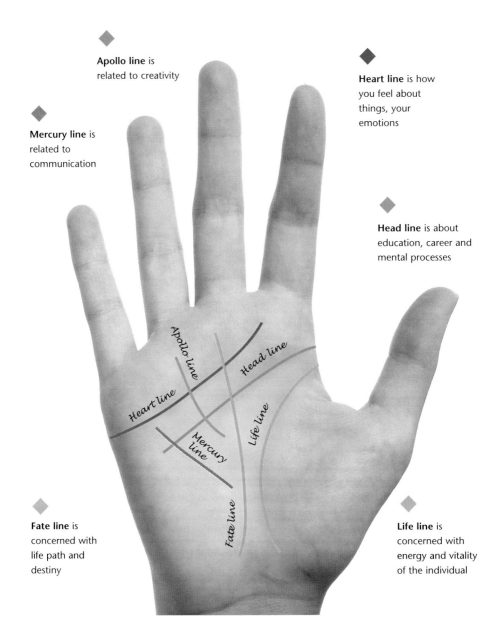

Apollo line is related to creativity

Heart line is how you feel about things, your emotions

Mercury line is related to communication

Head line is about education, career and mental processes

Fate line is concerned with life path and destiny

Life line is concerned with energy and vitality of the individual

the LIFE line

This line on your child's palm is of primary importance as it stands for health, constitution and prospects of longevity as well as some salient psychological factors.

The Life line normally begins under the base of the index or Jupiter finger, half way between the angle of the thumb with the hand and the base of the Jupiter finger. It then makes a curve around the ball of the child's thumb, towards the wrist. This is the first line to form in the fetal hand, very early on the first few months of development. This line has a lot to do with the life force and vitality of the individual. By its length, strength and clarity, you can get a clear indication of the vitality and energy to be anticipated in your child. The sweep of the Life line into the palm of your child's hand is very important; the greater the sweep, the larger will be your child's mount of Venus, which denotes a healthy appetite for life. If the angle created by the encircling of the Life line is small and narrow, it thus ensures a lesser mount of Venus and therefore a lack of life force and vitality. Children with the latter formation will have a certain apathy towards life and a disinclination to get active.

Based on her many years of thorough research, Beryl Hutchinson, the famous hand analyst, asserts that the Life line does not tell the length of life but it does have great bearing on the quality of life. It should, ideally, be strong and well marked and lack "islands", "chains", "tassels" or "breaks" (see The Marks on the Hand).

Where the Life line actually begins will also have a bearing on your child's drive and his or her sense of ambition. The Life line will always be influenced by its starting point (see overleaf).

If your child's Life line appears closely interwoven with her Head line at the beginning, it indicates that she will be inclined to be very sensitive about everything regarding herself.

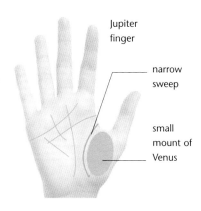

Jupiter finger

wide sweep

large mount of Venus

A wide curve
Your child will have a lot of vitality and drive and consequently a lot of energy to further his ambitions.

Jupiter finger

narrow sweep

small mount of Venus

A very narrow curve
Your child is lacking in vitality, energy and ambition.

Palmistry is full of old wives' tales and one such example concerns the Life line: "a long Life line means a long life, and a short Life line means a short life." I have not found this to be true as I have had many people with short Life lines come to see me and if the above were true, they'd never have reached my door!

where the Life line begins

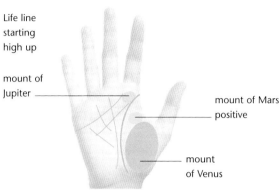

Life line starting high up

mount of Jupiter

mount of Mars positive

mount of Venus

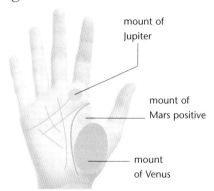

mount of Jupiter

mount of Mars positive

mount of Venus

High up on the hand

This Life line indicates ambition that develops very early, and children with this type of beginning to their Life lines are very difficult to hold back. Their minds mature early and they have strong competitive instincts, which manifest even in their early school years. If this line is very delicate and has lots of chains or islands, the early life of your child will be somewhat delicate and, due to her ambitious nature, she may be inclined to overdo things and lack the stamina to carry them through.

Between the mounts of Jupiter and Mars positive

This is the most common starting point of the Life line and indicates a good, strong early development in the child, unless it shows islands or chains. This type of line usually takes a wider curve around the mount of Venus than the others, and if it continues clear and well formed to the end, it is a strong sign of someone with a healthy constitution.

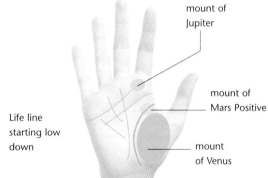

mount of Jupiter

mount of Mars Positive

Life line starting low down

mount of Venus

On the mount of Mars positive

This beginning can indicate a child who has an irritable temperament who can be quarrelsome and fretful. These children may be inclined to have difficulty with their peers. Children with this type of Life line may sometimes have a fascination with danger – wanting to play with knives or fire – and this needs close monitoring.

Her feelings are easily hurt as she is often self-centred and somewhat hesitant. She needs to be encouraged to fight against these traits and develop a sense of self-confidence and a healthy interest in others around her.

If your child has a distinct space between the beginning of his Life line and the beginning of his Head line, he is likely to be a child who likes to "have his head". He likes to be free to carry out his own plans and, if combined with an ambitious nature, he will strive for independence.

If your child has quite a large space between the beginnings of her Head and Life lines, she is a child who is inclined to be over-confident. She may have a tendency to be foolhardy, impetuous and a bit inclined to "run amok", particularly if her Life line begins on the mount of Mars. These children will sometimes develop a fascination with dangerous pursuits.

When the Life line forks at the end, in traditional palmistry this was always interpreted as an indication that the person would end up living in a foreign country, and I myself have invariably found this to be true.

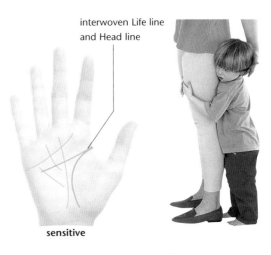

interwoven Life line and Head line

sensitive

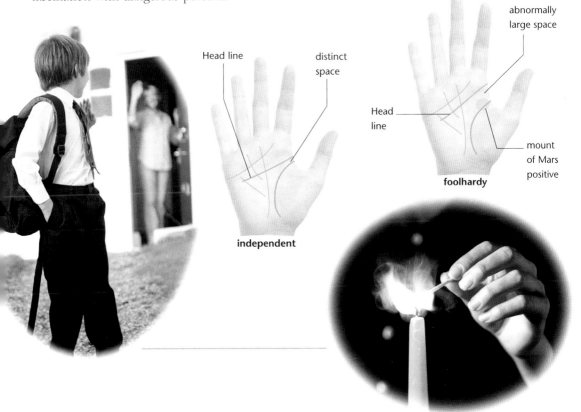

Head line

distinct space

independent

abnormally large space

Head line

mount of Mars positive

foolhardy

lines rising from the Life line

Towards Apollo finger and mount of Apollo

This is very often seen on the hands of children who, as adults, may become well known as media, political or sporting personalities. Children with this formation in their hand are hugely ambitious and have a certain charm, which endears them to the public. They have little fear of the limelight and love to bask in the sunlight of others' admiration. They rarely become arrogant; they just take it all in their stride as befits their sunny dispositions.

Towards the Saturn finger

This indicates a child who has ambitious tendencies but one who puts more laborious effort into what he is doing and makes hard work of it. This child can be a little over-critical of his own endeavours and have a lack of self-belief. A little praise now and then will help this child enormously.

Saturn finger

Jupiter finger

Apollo finger

Mount of Saturn

Apollo Saturn Jupiter

Travel lines

Life line

Towards the mount of Jupiter
Will indicate periods in a child's life when he has surges of increased drive and ambition.

Islands on any line (see page 65), indicate stress, and islands early on in the line will indicate that the child is overtaxing himself and that his ambition is outpacing his life energy.

Moving out from the Life line and down towards the wrist are usually referred to as "travel lines".

Guardian Angel line

Inside the Life line, running parallel with it, you can sometimes see another line. This is variously referred to as a double Life line, a Mars line, a Sister line or a Guardian Angel line.

My preference is to refer to this as a Guardian Angel line, as the possessor of it is most fortunate indeed. It seems to give to the owner extraordinary protection from the vicissitudes and trials and tribulations of life. The Guardian Angel line also gives the person extra physical strength and health. If your child has this line, she is very lucky.

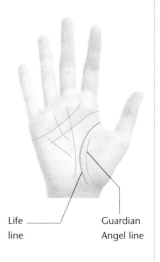

Life
line

Guardian
Angel line

All the major belief systems of the world teach that we each have a Guardian Angel or Guardian Spirit. I firmly believe this to be true. Although everyone has a Guardian Angel, those with a Guardian Angel line seem to be extra blessed. Even when they encounter problems, they always seem to be miraculously rescued.

I have seen many people who have this line and some have confirmed that they have had some remarkable escapes from accidents or that they have had extraordinary "lucky breaks". I've got one myself, and I have had several escapes from seriously dangerous situations. Having this line does not mean that your child will be in dangerous situations, only that he is more likely to escape from them, such as missing the plane that is going to crash. The lucky possessors of this line are also the ones who seem to be always taken care of, money turns up when they have none, or the right person always turns up when they need them.

the HEAD line

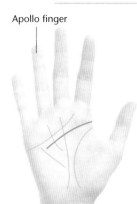

Apollo finger

This usually starts at the same point as the Life line. The Head line has great importance for the purpose of this book as it will give some more clues and indications as to the type of education and career path that your child should follow.

As with the Life line, the Head line should be clear and relatively unblemished. It should have a good depth and colour. The Head line usually cuts across through the middle of the palm, ending under the Apollo (ring) finger. According to Indian palmistry, when the Head line reaches the edge of the palm, the person will be successful using his mind. The Head line is sometimes referred to by certain palmists as a "mentality line", for the obvious reason that this line is to do with all things connected with the mind and the use of the mental faculties.

What is important about a sloping Head line is the type of hand that it is on. When a sloping Head line (sloping down towards the wrist) is on a Psychic/Sensitive or a Philosopher's hand then it is quite a different interpretation than when it is on the Square hand (see below).

If your child's Head line runs straight across his palm over to the opposite side of his hand, this little person will have a direct approach to matters in life and is one who "goes for it".

If your child's Head line is shorter than "normal" ("normal" is when it finishes under the Apollo finger), she is a child without a strong inner

direct

Psychic or Philosopher's hand
If the Head line slopes down on to the mount of Luna, he will be a child who has a great imagination, dreams a lot and is very visionary. This characteristic is generally found on the hands of would-be painters, writers, graphic designers, moviemakers or anyone who uses his imagination in his work. The sloping Head line enhances the values already determined on these types of hand.

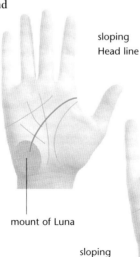

sloping
Head line

mount of Luna

sloping
Head line

Square hand
If the Head line slopes down on to the mount of Luna, this child will have some bright ideas, flashes of imagination and invention but will be prone to analyse things and be inclined to be far too practical. This may result in an internal clash, which is brought about by conflict between her imaginative, creative side and her practical side. The end result is likely to be that this child will manifest her creative skills in more practical ways.

where the Head line begins

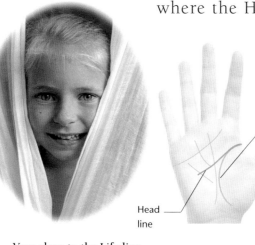

Life line

Head line

Very close to the Life line
If the Head and Life lines continue together for quite a while on the palm, this child may lack self-confidence and may have a fear of expressing his ideas and putting forward his views. He should be encouraged to believe in himself and, through receiving praise for his efforts, he will begin to see his own potential.

Independently of the Life line
If there is a little space in between the Head line and Life line and if the latter goes well across her hand, this denotes a strong streak of independence. Your child is a "free" thinker and is rarely bound by convention. She approaches things head on and has sufficient self-confidence to express even the most unusual views. Children like her aspire to fame and are likely to achieve status in some form of public service, the media or politics.

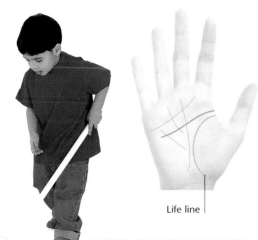

Life line

Inside Life line, on the mount of Mars positive
This child will have the Mars qualities of quarrelsomeness and argumentativeness and this will be intensified if the Head line runs straight across her hand to the other mount of Mars. Fortunately, this type of Head line is not common.

Life line

mount of Mars negative

mount of Mars positive

mount of Jupiter

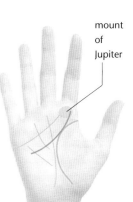

On mount of Jupiter
And if it descends towards and is slightly connected to the Life line, this indicates a marvellous quality of independence. Yet this child will usually also have the qualities of prudence and caution.

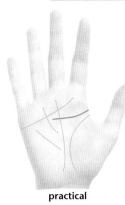

practical

vision. She likes practical, tangible things, and to know where she stands. She will prefer to do small jobs and to live a routine life and abide by the dictates of her social environment. However, you do always need to take other factors in the hand into consideration that may change your interpretation. A well-formed Jupiter finger or strong thumb will provide extra motivation.

If your child's Head line slopes up towards his Mercury (little) finger, he will be extremely good at expressing himself, either through written or spoken words.

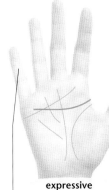

expressive

Mercury finger

branches on the Head line

There may be branches from the Head line on your child's hand; these are all significant depending on where the branch is heading.

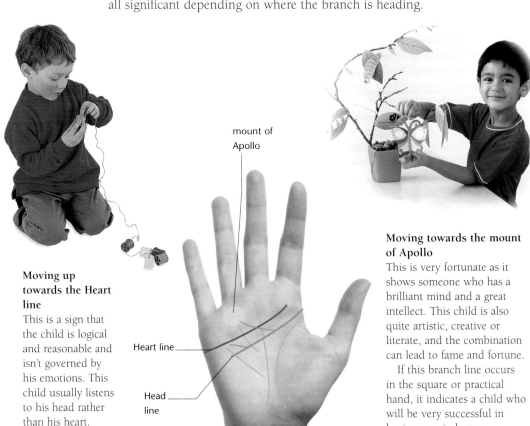

mount of Apollo

Heart line

Head line

Moving up towards the Heart line

This is a sign that the child is logical and reasonable and isn't governed by his emotions. This child usually listens to his head rather than his heart.

Moving towards the mount of Apollo

This is very fortunate as it shows someone who has a brilliant mind and a great intellect. This child is also quite artistic, creative or literate, and the combination can lead to fame and fortune.

If this branch line occurs in the square or practical hand, it indicates a child who will be very successful in business or industry.

marks on the Head line

There can be many different types of marks on your child's Head line (see also page 72). Very rarely, your child may have a double Head line on her hand. This indicates someone who will have significant success with money and will achieve economic greatness.

If there is **a square**, it is a positive sign of protection. Any squares on any line are a great thing to have.

If **little circles or triangles** appear, they are signs of preservation and protection from the vicissitudes of life.

A **star** is considered to be a very fortunate. Stars are indicative of lucky breaks and are sometimes even seen as signs of outstanding success.

An **island** is like a chain in a line. If you think of the line as a river, wherever there is an "island" in a river, it is a kind of obstruction. In palmistry, islands on the Head line are a warning that the child should be guarded against too much mental strain. Sometimes, parents are inclined to work their children beyond their capacity and drive them too hard. The island will disappear if a child is given the appropriate support at this stage.

If your child's Head line is composed of a **series of broken lines** instead of a clear unbroken one, it indicates a child who has a "stop-start" mentality. She'll do things then stop, then try again, then stop. She needs gentle discipline.

If there are **lots of islands** on the Head line and it begins to look like a chain, your child will definitely not blossom or flourish by being pushed. He needs to be led, guided, encouraged and supported. If he is driven too hard, he will collapse under the strain like a delicate flower.

Simian line

Sometimes in a hand you may see a line running right across it incorporating the Head line and Heart line – one line instead of two. This is called the Simian line and is frequently found in children with Down syndrome. However, those who have this line but are not Down syndrome children, are often of above-average intelligence and are highly focused, although they can be obsessive. They get "bees in their bonnets". They focus on a goal with almost tunnel-like vision and won't give up until they've reached it.

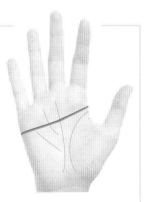

the HEART line

Your child's Heart line gives an indication of how she will respond emotionally to situations in life. This line portrays how she will relate to others and how her feelings will guide her.

At one time, only IQ (Intelligence Quotient) was taken into consideration when assessing a child's future success in life, but these days, his or her EQ (Emotional Quotient) is considered to be of equal importance. The whole person, rather than separate aspects of character, all come together to give a profile of the entire personality.

Your child's Heart line begins on the outside, or percussion side of his hand – that is the side opposite the thumb. It gently curves across the hand towards the mount of Jupiter. Like all lines it should be well formed, deep and have a good colour and continuity.

The Heart line relates to emotions and affairs of the heart, rather than to the physical heart. If this line is the most prominent in your child's hand, it denotes a personality who is likely to allow the emotional side of his nature to overshadow other aspects of his life. He may be inclined to act impulsively, without considering the consequences.

We need not go into too much detail regarding this line in a book concerned with children, except that the Heart line is very important to how your child will relate to other people. This will greatly affect her career opportunities and her relationships with peers, schoolmates and workplace colleagues.

When the Heart line lies straight across the palm it denotes a child who is sincere, honest and affectionate. He isn't likely to be swayed by any great emotions one way or the other.

If the line curves down towards his Head line, this is a child who needs constant reassurance and has an extreme need for love. Taken together with other signs in the hand, such as a little finger that leans towards the other fingers, this particular child will need a lot of encouragement and

percussion side — mount of Jupiter

sincere

Head line

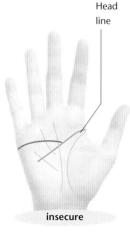

insecure

approval. A few hugs wouldn't go amiss!

If your child's Heart line finishes on his mount of Jupiter, he will be very reliable in his love nature and has the potential to take great care of those who work with or for him. He is protective towards others and expansive in nature. Consequently, he would find working in hospitality or the caring professions agreeable. But, as ever, other aspects of the hand must be taken into account when making a complete analysis.

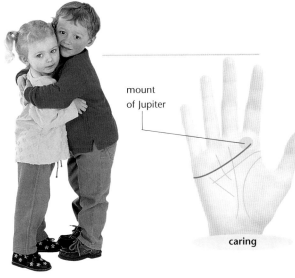

mount of Jupiter

caring

If your child's Heart line finishes on her mount of Saturn, she is very self-contained and will have a great sense of duty. In adult life, she would do well when working for a cause, as she would be inclined to show loyalty to a noble career. This type of personality will usually have a calling for what she does and would make a good teacher, minister or soldier. Her sense of duty gives her the desire to work for King and Country or for a worthy cause.

When the Heart line runs very close the Head line, this child will have difficulty in keeping affairs of the heart and head separate.

A child with a Heart line with one branch finishing on the mount of Jupiter and another finishing between the first and second fingers will be likely to have a very balanced disposition.

If your child's Heart line is thin, fine and weak it indicates a child who is not inclined to "put his heart into" things; he can be a little on the "wishy-washy" side.

Remember, when studying the hand it is important to take all other signs in the hand into consideration before making sweeping generalizations.

dutiful

mount of Saturn

Head line

emotional

Saturn finger

Jupiter finger

mount of Jupiter

balanced

wishywashy

the APOLLO or SUN line

This is also called the line of Success. It very often begins in the centre of the palm and travels up towards the Apollo finger.

Traditional palmists would have said that having this line was a guarantee of success or fame, but today's hand analysts are more inclined to see it as an indication of creative talent. The line is generally more clearly shown on the Psychic/Sensitive or Philosopher's Hand but it can be seen on the Square or Spatulate Hand.

This line is not present in every hand, but when it is, it is an indication of an inner happiness and contentment which are, after all, the only real measures of success. A child with this line will have a great capacity to enjoy life and thus derive happiness from a career that he loves.

It is frequently found starting from the Head line. Wherever it begins, the termination point is on the mount of Apollo. Having this line is extremely fortuitous. It seems to increase the good qualities of a child who has a good Fate lines and it gives improvements in other areas of life.

If there are any adverse lines in the hand, the Apollo line will modify them as it is the "sunshine after the rain" syndrome.

If the line is weak or patchy, it indicates that success may be intermittent, sometimes because of a lack of concentration or staying power and sometimes because of a lack of opportunity.

Multiple Apollo lines indicate a child who is versatile and multi-talented. He is often gifted in several areas and will achieve success and satisfaction from all his many interests.

mount of Apollo

where the Apollo line begins

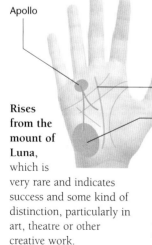

mount of Apollo

Fate line

mount of Luna

Heart line

Head line

Rises from the mount of Luna, which is very rare and indicates success and some kind of distinction, particularly in art, theatre or other creative work.

From the Fate line
This indicates that the child will be successful, as it is his destiny. If this Apollo line rises up to the mount of Apollo, it denotes success which is achieved through hard work and dedication.

From the Heart line
This can indicate great love in a child's life, or a great talent for creating beautiful things. For this child, particularly as an adult, it indicates a great deal of sunshine and happiness.

From the Head line
This indicates success when that child is using his head.

the FATE line

Sometimes called the line of Destiny or Career line, the Fate line starts and runs from the direction of the wrist up towards the second or Saturn finger.

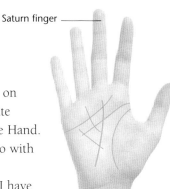

Saturn finger

When examining this line, it is important to look at the type of hand on which it is found. It isn't usually very obvious on a Square or Spatulate Hand, but is more often found on a Philosopher's or Psychic/Sensitive Hand.

Some followers of Eastern philosophy believe that this line is to do with one's karma – lessons we have to learn in this lifetime.

In my studies and research of thousands of hands over the years, I have found that owners of a strong Fate line very much enjoy working for themselves. They like to do their own thing; if they can't, they must be in charge and have control over their own actions. They aren't followers.

When the Fate line rises more on the mount of Luna, that person likes to travel; if she can't travel geographically, she travels mentally by exploring unusual ideas and philosophies. This person can be quite fortunate.

When the Fate line has a break in it, it is often a sign of a major break in the career. It will indicate a change of direction, usually to do something quite different to that which was done previously.

When it begins on the mount of Venus, this person will have a great love of the good life. He is well suited to a career that allows him to enjoy good food, good wine, and good living, like a restaurant critic or hotelier.

Children who have no Fate line on their hands, can still be very successful provided their Head lines are well-marked and there are other favourable signs in the hand such as an extra-long Jupiter finger.

mount of Venus

mount of Luna

traveller

gourmand

where the Fate line ends

Apollo Saturn Jupiter

Straight up towards the mount of Saturn
This person is usually successful in life though application and dedication; this is an individual who has a sense of duty.

Towards the mount of Apollo
Or if a branch of it is going towards this mount, there is a promise of success or unusual achievement or recognition in the person's public life.

Up to the mount of Jupiter
There is a certain element of good luck or fortune for this person.

the MERCURY or HEALTH line

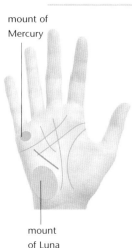

mount of
Mercury

mount
of Luna

The Mercury or Health line begins at the base of the palm and works upwards to the Mercury or little finger, or it starts at the mount of Luna and goes towards the mount of Mercury. It is a straight line.

In the past, it was believed that this line indicated problems with health; some old hand analysts actually referred to it as a Hepatica (after liver) line. My own experience of this line is that I have noticed it on the hands of those who have allergies or food sensitivities. I have noted, too, that those who possess this line, maybe because of their own experiences, seem to have an interest in health issues. They may be drawn to careers as health practitioners or dieticians.

Intuition line

This line can sometimes be confused with the Mercury line, but whereas the Mercury line is straight, the Intuition line is curved. It begins on the mount of Luna and goes towards the mount of Mercury. Children with this line will be extremely sensitive, possibly psychic and almost certainly clairvoyant. They will be aware of their surroundings and of people; they often will be vulnerable and sensitive. This line can be very useful in the hands of those who work with people such as counsellors, healers and therapists and those who work in the fields of personal growth or self-improvement.

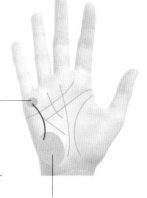

mount of
Mercury

mount
of Luna

A person who has this line will find working in the business world difficult. His sensitive nature will make it hard for him to handle the cut-throat attitudes of business. However, the Intuition line has a positive side in business in that it can keep the individual one step ahead of colleagues because it gives him a strong intuition.

Unusual marks

Stars

This is an asterisk-like mark on the hand and is very favourable, depending, of course, on where in the hand it is found.

On the mount of Saturn
A star here indicates someone who can achieve high status in public office, often with a certain sacrifice to his private life. It is as if the child has a destiny to fulfill, bringing him to high prominence but at a cost to family life or other interests.

High up on the mount of Jupiter
A star close to the base of the Jupiter finger indicates great success for the child in whatever endeavour she engages.

On the mount of Apollo
A star here indicates great success especially in artistic fields. It also promises great riches but the possessors of it usually have unsettled dispositions; they are never totally satisfied with what they've achieved – they always want to achieve more.

Lower down on the mount of Jupiter
A star here means your child will come into contact with famous and influential people, thus she will have a certain amount of influence herself.

On the mount of Mars positive
A star here often indicates a child who can have a distinguished military career or who will make a name for himself as a crusader – such as a worker with Amnesty International or Greenpeace, or in a revolutionary pursuit.

mount of Saturn

mount of Jupiter

mount of Apollo

mount of Mercury

mount of Mars positive

mount of Venus

On the mount of Mercury
A star here indicates someone who will have success in the field of communications. It is sometimes a promise of distinction in a money-making career, particularly if the Head line lies straight across the hand right underneath it.

On the mount of Venus
A prominent star indicates a child with great personal magnetism; she will have a lot of friends, be successful in love and will have a busy social calendar. She is popular and people love to have her around.

Crosses

Towards the base of the palm, between the mounts of Luna and Venus, lies another mount, the mount of Neptune (see below). If the mount of Neptune features a cross, this is sometimes referred to as St. Andrew's Cross or the Life Saving Cross, but is best known as the Healing Cross.

Under the Saturn or middle finger, in the space between the Heart and Head lines sometimes you can see a Mystic Cross.

The Mystic Cross

When well-defined, it shows a child who has an interest in the mystical way of life and is the possessor of true mediumistic and clairvoyant abilities. This child can "see round corners", which is useful in any walk of life but it is particularly useful in the hands of those who wish to work with people. It enables the individual to guide others through life's trials and tribulations.

Such careers as psychic consultant, intuitive healer, diagnostician, counsellor, psychotherapist or life coach would suit this child.

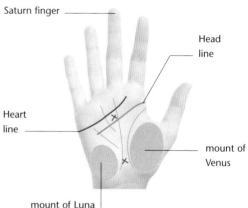

The Healing Cross

When you find this cross in the hand it's good to look at other areas of the hand to determine for which particular field of healing this child would be suitable. If the Healing Cross is found in the hand of a child with a Teacher's Square (see opposite), she would be able to heal someone by teaching him how to have a better way of life. In this case, a career in personal- growth or teaching self awareness would be appropriate.

A child with this cross will be someone with the potential to become a healer. The word "heal" comes from the old English and means to make whole or to fix, so this cross will be found in the hands of "people fixers", whether it is in the area of medical, psychological or any form of work that helps other people to make their lives complete.

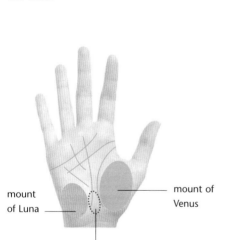

The mount of Neptune

Hardly a mount, it is the space just above the wrist and between the mount of Venus and the mount of Luna.

Squares

Squares anywhere on the hand indicate protection in that particular area.

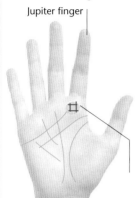

Jupiter finger

mount of Jupiter

The Teacher's Square

The square under the Jupiter finger, right on the mount of Jupiter, is often referred to as the Teacher's Square. This indicates someone who would be good as an educator of some kind, perhaps as a coach or personal trainer, bearing in mind other indications in the hand that would support this career path. If a child with a Teacher's Square doesn't go into a teaching career, he will often be a person who will teach in everyday life but will teach by example and by his achievements.

Medical stigmata

On the mount of Mercury, underneath the Mercury or little finger, you may find three parallel lines, referred to as the Medical stigmata.

Mercury finger

mount of Mercury

These lines indicate someone who would do extremely well in any field of healing. As the lines are under the Mercury finger, it usually indicates a child who can achieve results through his communication skills. One palmist has recently named these lines "Samaritan" lines, so the bearer of these lines would be a good counsellor and should consider a career that entails listening to others' problems and helping them shift their beliefs and attitudes. Becoming a Samaritan, healer, psychologist, or social worker would be suitable. When a line cuts a cross through these three lines, it can indicate the potential for a child to enter the medical profession either as a surgeon, dentist or someone who uses instruments in the performance of his work.

Marriage and children lines

As this book is primarily targeted at parents of younger children who want to help guide their children towards a fulfilling career, the discussion of these lines is inappropriate. There are many books that focus on this aspect of the hand.

Ring of Solomon

mount of Jupiter

The ring of Solomon forms a semi-circle across the mount of Jupiter at the base of the Jupiter or index finger. It will normally start halfway between the beginning of the Life line and the crease of the Jupiter finger and works it ways across the mount of Jupiter.

The Ring of Solomon represents wisdom and if your child has this ring, she will usually have great innate wisdom; it is as if she was born with it and she has chosen to share this wisdom with others throughout her lifetime. It seems to be her fate and destiny to do so.

This child will do very well in any career where wisdom is required, bearing in mind that wisdom and knowledge are entirely different qualities: knowledge can be learned; wisdom is something one is born with or acquires through adversity.

Jupiter finger

Life line

Girdle of Venus

mount of Apollo

This begins between the Jupiter (index) and Saturn (middle) fingers, curves gently across the mounts of Saturn and Apollo and finishes up between the Apollo (ring) and Mercury (little) fingers.

When it is clear, flawless and well-formed it indicates someone who has a highly developed sense of aesthetics, loves beauty and tries to create beauty around him.

When this line is ill formed, broken or sometimes found double, it indicates someone who goes over the top. He is inclined to extreme behaviour, whether it takes the shape of over-exercising, over-eating or, indeed, over-working.

mount of Saturn

The Droplets

These are fleshy pads on the tips of the fingers.

These indicate a child who is very tactile. She experiences the world through the heightened sense of touch. She loves to feel fabrics, wood, silk and earth, and to get her hands into things.

If your child has signs of healing in her hands as well – such as the St. Andrew's Cross or Medical stigmata – this will indicate strong hands-on healing abilities. This is particularly magnified if your child has circular fingerprint patterns on these droplets. It is almost as if the healing energy coming down through her arms wants to burst out of the tips of her fingers!

The Writer's Fork

Apollo
finger

Head
line

Sometimes the Head line will have another branch which breaks off and runs down to the mount of Luna. This is commonly known as the Writer's Fork.

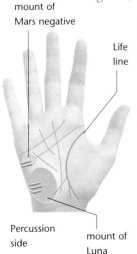

This sign indicates a child who can express herself well through the written or spoken word. This is especially so when the Writer's Fork is under the Apollo finger and slopes towards the mount of Luna. Ideally, a budding writer would have a spatulate tip to her Mercury finger.

A Writer's Fork can also indicate a child who has a sense of drama or a theatrical bent, leading to a career in acting, theatre work, window-dressing or designing.

If your child has a Writer's Fork and her hand has square tipped fingers, she will have an ability to organize ideas.

If you think that your child has budding literary talents, encourage her to keep a journal recording her thoughts, dreams and daily observations. Always make sure that she has plenty to read and encourage her to read books rather than watch television. The more your child reads, the better her vocabulary and, as she reads, she will automatically absorb correct spellings.

Mercury
finger

mount
of Luna

If your child's hand is limp and malleable, he may dream of writing or acting, but never actually achieve it.

Travel Lines

If your child has lines which begin at the percussion side, or outside, of the hand and run across the mount of Luna, or are on the mount of Mars negative, she is likely to have the desire to travel the world.

mount of
Mars negative

Life
line

The more lines, the more journeys. In these days of much travel, these lines are not as unusual as they might once have been. The longer and stronger the lines, the more important the journey, and those who are likely to become explorers or adventure travellers will usually have many of these lines.

Strong lines running down from the Life line to the mount of Luna also can be indicative of long voyages or meaningful journeys. When the Life line itself divides at the end, this has been traditionally seen as an indication that the person would end up living in a foreign country, rather that just visiting.

If a child with these lines is unable to travel, he is likely to get very frustrated. However, even if he can't travel physically, he can get a great deal of satisfaction from reading or travelling through the inner realms of the mind.

Percussion
side

mount of
Luna

Hand stories

Every hand tells a unique and fascinating tale, if only you knew how to read it! Learn how to take your child's print and meet some of the very interesting hands and children of my acquaintance.

making a HAND print

Almost all the features of your child's hand can be captured in an ink print. This can be useful if you need to study your child's hand for some while (as children will rarely want to sit still for very long) or, until you become more proficient at hand reading, if you want to compare the marks on her hand with those in this book. Keeping a record of your child's hand through yearly prints is also a fun thing to do.

YOU WILL NEED
Water-soluble printing ink
Sheet of glass or laminated plastic
10-cm (4-in) printer's roller
Sheets of paper
Pencil with sharp point, or pen
Newspapers to protect surface
Washing-up liquid to clean up!

1 **Squeeze a small amount of ink** onto the sheet of glass or plastic. Make sure the surface underneath is well protected.

2 **Roll out the ink** with the roller so that the ink coats the roller's rubber part evenly. The ink doesn't have to be spread too widely.

3 **Thoroughly coat the hand** with the ink, making sure you go all the way up to the fingertips and down to the wrist.

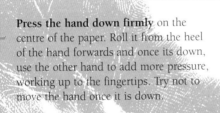

4 **Press the hand down firmly** on the centre of the paper. Roll it from the heel of the hand forwards and once its down, use the other hand to add more pressure, working up to the fingertips. Try not to move the hand once it is down.

5 **Draw around** the hand, down to the wrist, with a pencil or pen to create an outline and then lift the hand in one movement so as not to smudge the print.

6 **The finished print** will contain all the lines and marks but may not show the thumb to advantage. You can make a separate print of this. Make sure to write the date on the paper.

EVA's hand

EVA has quite a long narrow palm; this indicates a child who thinks deeply about things. When she held her hands out to be read, I noticed that she held her little, or Mercury, finger away from the others; this indicates someone who likes her own company and wants occasionally to get away from the crowd. In fact, she will actually need her space from time to time, as other indications in her hand show that she will be someone who will want to give a great deal of herself to others.

A lot of fine lines on the palm indicate great sensitivity and a tendency to worry about many things. This is a thoughtful and caring child, which is borne out by many other indications in her hand, such as The Healing Cross. When I see this in a hand, I immediately look for other signs to show me which of the many forms of healing the possessor could follow. Eva has a choice: she has the "droplets" on the tips of her fingers,

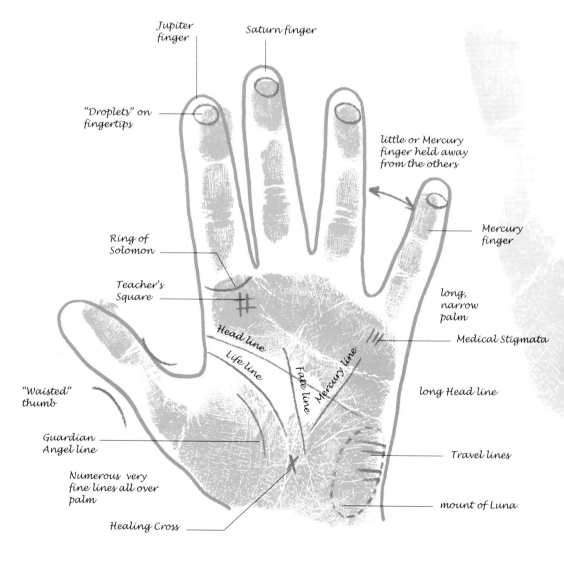

Jupiter finger

Saturn finger

"Droplets" on fingertips

little or Mercury finger held away from the others

Mercury finger

Ring of Solomon

Teacher's Square

long, narrow palm

Medical Stigmata

Head line

Life line

Fate line

Mercury line

"Waisted" thumb

long Head line

Guardian Angel line

Travel lines

Numerous very fine lines all over palm

mount of Luna

Healing Cross

which would allow her to follow a touch type of healing, such as aromatherapy, reiki, osteopathy, or some other form of hands-on therapy, and she also has the Medical stigmata or Samaritan lines, which would allow her to have a career as a counsellor.

Under Eva's Jupiter finger is the Teacher's Square and she also has a Ring of Solomon. (The latter does not show in the hand-print but was clearly visible on personal examination). The Ring of Solomon shows someone with a high degree of innate wisdom and this, combined with her Teacher's Square, would indicate that Eva could become a very good workshop facilitator in something like the field of personal development or self awareness. As she also has The Healing Cross, what better way for Eva to heal people than to empower them

through teaching them or enabling them to make more of their lives?

Eva's unusually long Head line shows a child who will do well using her brain. Her Fate line, which starts on her mount of Luna and runs up toward her Saturn finger, shows she will take her obligations seriously and have a good dedication to duty and to "doing the right thing". Eva also has a "waisted" thumb, showing her concern to get things just right. She would benefit from a lot of reassurance as to her own self worth.

Inside her Life line, she has a nice Guardian Angel line, so she is always protected and safe. This is good, as there are many travel lines in Eva's hand. I would be surprised if Eva did not travel the world as some well-known teacher dispensing her wisdom!

Possible careers for Eva

SEMINAR LEADER

COUNSELLOR

life coach

TEACHER

wisdom guru

BEN's hand

I had the pleasure of seeing Ben's hand and examining it in person. Actually, seeing and holding the hand is by far the most accurate way of making a judgment, rather than just looking at a hand-print.

Ben held his hand out to be read in a very open and confident manner; this shows a child who is open and gregarious. His palm is a good example of the square palm, and combined with his spatulate fingertips, this makes him a very interesting little character. The square palm would immediately mark Ben out as practical and down-to-earth, but then when you take other characteristics in his palm into consideration, he comes across as a much more complex individual.

Ben's fingers are spatulate, which marks him as having great creative potential. The square palm would then mean that Ben's creativity is of a practical nature. Combined with a very pronounced mount of Luna (this is not apparent on his print, but I saw it in actuality), Ben is capable putting his dreams and his "castles in the air" into practical form.

I was also able to examine Ben's nails, which were quite short; this indicates a sense of impatience, of wanting to get on with things. There is a pronounced space between the start of Ben's Life line and Head line. This indicates a desire to be very independent and not have to "toe-the-line". Ben will always strive for independence.

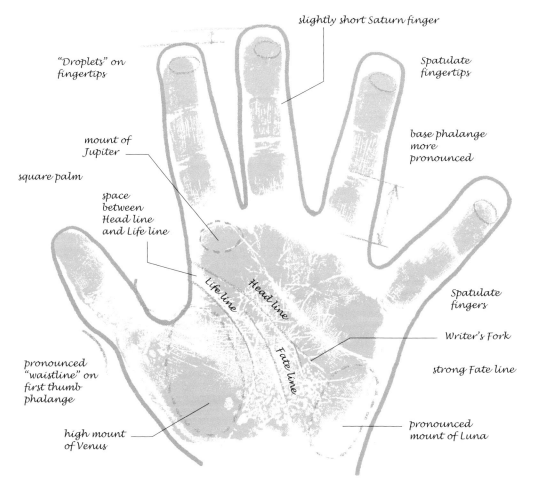

slightly short Saturn finger

"Droplets" on fingertips

Spatulate fingertips

mount of Jupiter

square palm

base phalange more pronounced

space between Head line and Life line

Life line

Head line

Spatulate fingers

Writer's Fork

Fate line

pronounced "waistline" on first thumb phalange

strong Fate line

high mount of Venus

pronounced mount of Luna

His Head line slopes down towards his mount of Luna and, in Ben's square hand, this will give him flashes of imagination and creative insights. However, the squareness of the palm will cause him to analyze things and this will produce a certain amount of conflict between his practical and imaginative sides. Ben also has a nice "Writer's Fork" at the end of his Head line. It does not necessarily mean that he will write, but he will be full of ideas and be quite good at expressing them.

Ben's Fate line is of particular interest. Strong Fate lines are not often found on the Square palm. In my experience, I have found that owners of strong Fate lines generally like to work for themselves. Ben's Fate line runs from his mount of Luna towards his Life line and under his mount of Jupiter. Ben's parents would do well to guide Ben towards a vocation with a creative emphasis, as the mount of Luna rules the imagination and inner landscapes.

Ben also has a high mount of Venus, showing a child who loves the physical pleasures of life.

I'm told he loves lots of chocolate! The base phalanges of Ben's fingers are more developed than the others; this marks him out as someone who loves his home comforts. The "Droplets" on the tips of his fingers (again not evident on the print but very evident on close examination) indicate someone who is quite tactile and will get a lot of impressions from his sense of touch.

Ben has a quite pronounced "waistline" on the first phalange of his thumb; this reveals a child with a sense of self-criticism and a desire to achieve perfection – not a bad thing if he is to follow a creative career, as what he creates will, no doubt, be as perfect as he can make it.

Ben's Saturn finger seems to be just slightly short, which means that he will not be of a too serious or saturnine disposition. He may lean towards a bohemian lifestyle but his Square palm will ensure that he completes all the projects that he has begun.

Possible careers for Ben

ARCHITECT

CHEF

landscape architect

FASHION, INTERIOR OR SET DESIGNER

BRONTE's hand

Bronte has a very long and quite narrow hand, which indicates sensitivity and conscientiousness. It also means that she has a strong ability to concentrate. The hand is quite "fluid" in the sense that it is quite malleable to touch. There is quite a bit of movement in Bronte's hands and a great flexibility of physique.

Bronte has a quite high and pronounced mount of Luna, showing her well-developed imagination.

When I pushed against Bronte's thumb (without her expecting me to), it went right back, which shows a lack of assertiveness. Her thumb is also "waisted" revealing a lot of self-criticism and feelings of not being good enough.

The general fineness of the skin and texture of Bronte's hand show a sensitive constitution and a sensitive personality. She is shy and very aware. This fineness of the hand shows a child who dislikes grossness of any kind and loves beauty in her environment. The tips of her fingers are slightly spatulate, indicating a degree of creativity. This creativity, coupled with her well-developed imagination, would indicate someone with great inner vision.

Bronte has a Writer's Fork at the end of her Head line. This does not always mean writing as such, but any form of artistic expression. With

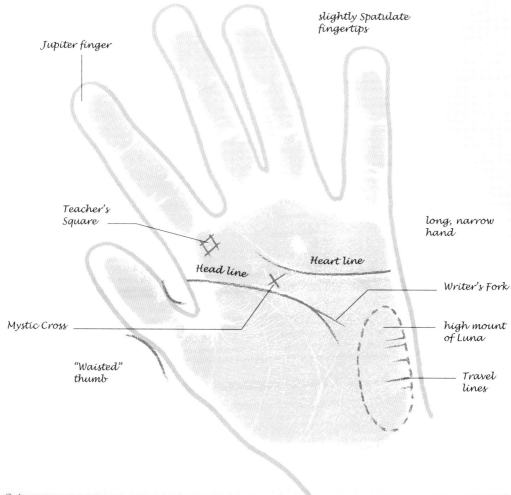

slightly spatulate fingertips

Jupiter finger

Teacher's Square

long, narrow hand

Heart line

Head line

Writer's Fork

Mystic Cross

high mount of Luna

"Waisted" thumb

Travel lines

Bronte's fluidity of movement, acting or dancing would be an option. She also has a Teacher's Square in her hand, so she could teach dancing or physical movement such as *T'ai Chi*.

There are also many travel lines in Bronte's hand. This can indicate actual travel or, with Bronte's strong inner vision, travel in the realms of the imagination. Bronte can be very happy with her own company and will probably spend a lot of happy times playing alone.

Bronte is also quite psychic as evidenced by the shape of her hand and her high mount of Luna. She possesses a Mystic Cross between her Head and Heart lines. She may be one of those lucky people who can see realities not available to the rest of the world. She is inclined to be a dreamer. Unfortunately, dreaming is not encouraged in our education system; more's the pity I think, because it is in dreaming that composers get their ideas, as do writers, inventors and architects. So, carry on dreaming!

FRIENDS
Bronte and Jasmine (page 86), two delightful little girls, are devoted friends. It was interesting to look at their hands from the point of view of their friendship, as they were quite unalike. Their friendship really bears out the theory that opposites attract – being drawn to in others what we do not have in ourselves. There is never going to be too much rivalry and each will admire in the other the traits that she herself does not possess. Jasmine and Bronte complement each other beautifully. They can learn different things from one another.

Possible careers for Bronte

dancer

ACTRESS

TEACHER OF DANCE OR MOVEMENT

VISIONARY

psychic

JASMINE's hand

Comparing Jasmine's right and left hands, which were very similar, shows me a very well-balanced little girl. The length of her palm and the length of her hand are also well balanced. Jasmine's palm is quite wide, showing someone who has a broad and positive outlook on life. This also indicates an innate sympathy and a generous nature. She held her hand out to me with the fingers splayed out, showing a gregarious nature. She is someone who mixes well and gets on well with people. Her high mounts of Luna and Venus show a romantic and a sensualist.

When I first examined Jasmine's hand, she held her thumb well away from her palm, at more than a 45° angle. This shows confidence and a strong streak of individuality. She will need careful guidance and discipline. When I pressed against Jasmine's thumb, it held strong against me, showing a strong will and sense of determination.

Jasmine's Mercury finger is long and well formed, showing someone who can talk well and will be able to talk her way in and out of any situation. Jasmine's Head line forks, also indicating a good ability to express her many ideas. Her Fate line is strong, and is well connected to her Head line. She is fated to use her head.

Possible careers for Jasmine

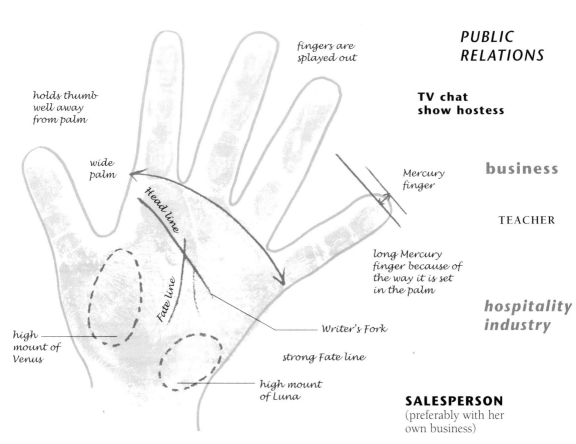

fingers are splayed out

PUBLIC RELATIONS

TV chat show hostess

holds thumb well away from palm

wide palm

Head line

Mercury finger

business

TEACHER

long Mercury finger because of the way it is set in the palm

Fate line

high mount of Venus

Writer's Fork

strong Fate line

high mount of Luna

hospitality industry

SALESPERSON
(preferably with her own business)

IONA's hand

AGE: 8 **right-handed**

Iona has a square and broad palm with quite short fingers. The Square palm gives her a practical side and the short fingers show a quick-thinking mind. When I pressed against Iona's thumb, she resisted the pressure quite well, indicating assertiveness and a strong will. Her thumb was also held well out from the palm at an angle of at least 45°; this shows good leadership qualities and the potential to be a "mover and a shaker". Iona's mount of Jupiter was well developed and high, indicating leadership and individuality. Her hand looks generally robust and the Life line is strong and well formed, sweeping in a wide arc out into the palm. These are all good indications of drive and ambition.

Iona's Life and Head lines are separate, which indicates a person who likes her independence and who won't be too tempted to conform. Her Head line begins on the mount of Jupiter, showing someone who has bags of self confidence and may express unusual views. She is likely to aspire to fame and be successful in some form of public life, such as the media or politics.

Iona's Fate line moves towards her Saturn finger, which shows a certain adherence to the principles of duty. This is in contradiction to her aforementioned independent streak and may cause her to have a certain amount of inner conflict in her life.

Iona has a very definite bump on the percussion side of her hand. This indicates an adventurous nature. It is said that Scott of the Antarctic had just such a bump. I have not been able to verify this, but have seen many adventurers' hands that had just such a bump. One was on the hand of a man who travelled to all kinds of wild and inaccessible places to make television documentaries.

Iona's Heart line is well placed between her Jupiter and Saturn fingers. This shows someone who has a good sense of self and yet also has a sense of responsibility towards others..

Possible careers for Iona

TRAVEL

POLITICS

conservationist

hospitality industry

EXPLORER

SALES

ENTREPRENEUR

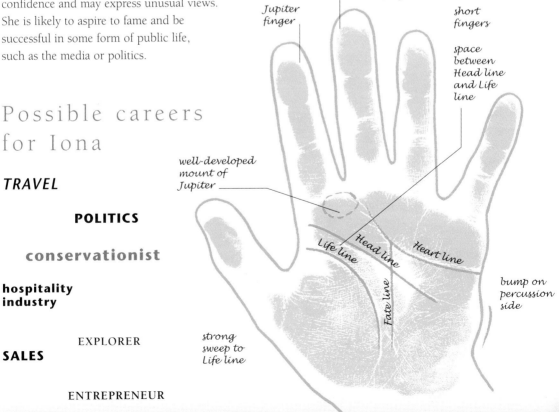

Jupiter finger

Saturn finger

short fingers

space between Head line and Life line

well-developed mount of Jupiter

Life line

Head line

Heart line

Fate line

strong sweep to Life line

bump on percussion side

HARRIET's hand

Harriet's hand falls into a combination of the Mixed and the Philosopher's hand types, as her hands are long and her finger joints, or knuckles, quite pronounced. The finger shapes are mixed. When I asked her to resist the pressure I put on her thumb, it was strong, indicating a strong will and a sense of determination.

Her long fingers, with their wide knuckle joints, indicate a thoughtful personality, tending towards a philosophical approach to life.

Her strong Fate line, moving towards the mount of Saturn (does not show very clearly on hand-print) indicates someone with a sense of justice and order. She has the "waisted" thumb, which shows an inclination to analyze herself and others. There is a tendency to demand

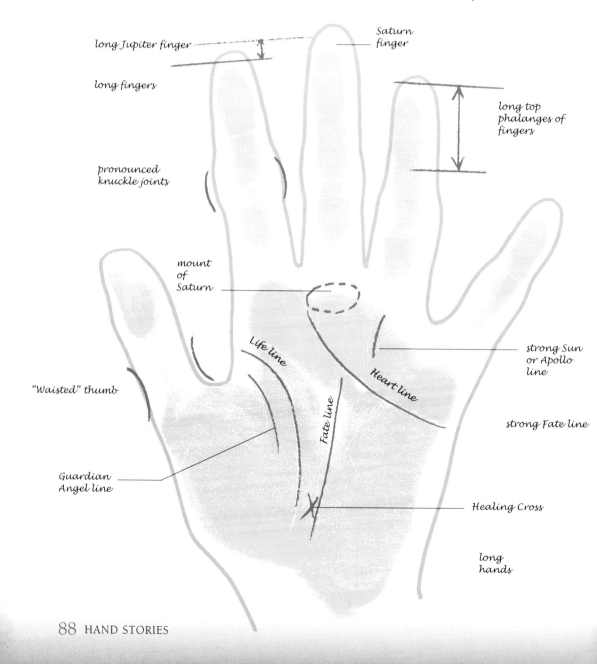

long Jupiter finger

Saturn finger

long fingers

long top phalanges of fingers

pronounced knuckle joints

mount of Saturn

Life line

"Waisted" thumb

Heart line

strong Sun or Apollo line

Fate line

strong Fate line

Guardian Angel line

Healing Cross

long hands

perfection from herself – an unachievable goal for anyone! Harriet will always strive to reach truth and justice.

Harriet also has a strong Sun or Apollo line, which is indicative of her potential for success in life. Some would say it is indicative of luck, but I believe that we make our own luck, and Harriet certainly has the tools and ability to do so. She also has a love of beautiful things and a strong sense of aesthetics. Some creative activity would be a good hobby for Harriet; it would be a good release and escape from the restrictions of the life of service and duty that her hand indicates she might be involved in.

Harriet's Jupiter finger is long in proportion to her other fingers; this indicates the potential to be a good leader. Her Heart line, nicely ending between her Jupiter and Saturn fingers, shows someone who respects herself and has respect and concern for others.

Harriet has a clear Guardian Angel line on her hand, showing that she is always safe and divinely protected. She also has the Healing Cross, which denotes that she likes to help others, or to heal people or situations.

There are many travel lines on Harriet's hand.

The top phalange of her fingers is quite long; showing someone who has the potential to develop a strong sense of spirituality or spiritual values. Spiritual is not to be confused with religious.

Interestingly, when I asked Harriet what she would like to do, her answer was that she would like to be a lawyer. This was before I suggested possible careers for her. Here is a young lady with a strong sense of her mission in life!

Possible careers for Harriet

ETHICAL POLITICIAN

LAWYER

arbitrator

JUDGE

involvement in conflict resolution

Jordan's hand

AGE: 7   right-handed

Jordan put his hand so squarely on the paper that it shows someone with a great degree of confidence. The wide spaces between all of his digits reveals someone who is outgoing and gregarious.

The angle at which Jordan's thumb is held shows a strong character and a pronounced individuality. The thumb's base or first phalange has quite a pronounced "waistline" to it, which shows that he can be a perfectionist and will query his own performance, despite his confidence. This is not a bad thing, as this will temper Jordan's desire to be in control.

Jordan has a square palm and square fingertips, which show a practical creativity. The base phalanges of his fingers are well padded and fleshed out, which shows a great desire to enjoy the creature comforts of life. The square palmed practicality, however, is counterbalanced by his high and well developed mount of Luna; this gives him a lot of sensitivity and a very vivid imagination. Despite the gregariousness shown by his widely spaced fingers,

Jordan has the gift of imagination and is very happy retreating into his own inner world at times – no doubt a beautiful and magical place!

Note how Jordan's Head line practically dives down towards his mount of Luna. This shows a great imagination and maybe a love of the mysterious and the unexplained. I also note a Mystic Cross between his Head and Heart lines, which shows that he may have a great desire to understand the mystical aspects of life. However, with the practical squareness of his palm and fingers he will not become "airy fairy".

His Fate line starts at the Life line and moves to the mount of Saturn. This shows someone with a deeply felt mission of some kind. Maybe a desire to help the world in some way.

He also has the Healing Cross; factor this in with his Mystic Cross and gregariousness, and Jordan may indeed make his mark in some effort where he will make a contribution to the world. He has all the energy and determination to do so. One thing is sure, Jordan will not easily be TOLD what to do; he responds better when given choices.

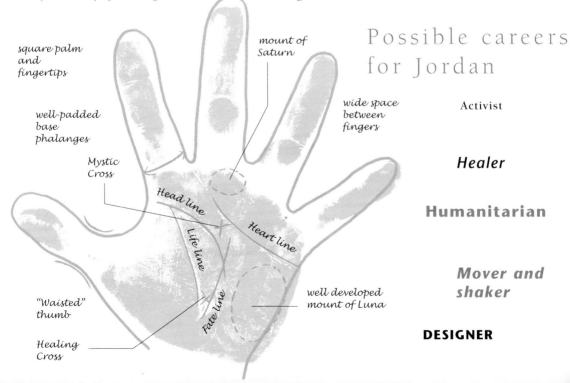

square palm and fingertips

well-padded base phalanges

Mystic Cross

Head line

Life line

Heart line

mount of Saturn

wide space between fingers

"Waisted" thumb

Fate line

well developed mount of Luna

Healing Cross

Possible careers for Jordan

Activist

Healer

Humanitarian

Mover and shaker

DESIGNER

TWINS

Max and Lucie are twins and very often one twin is left-handed and one right-handed. One is also usually stronger, more confident and manipulative than the other. But overall, the information gained through my reading gave a deeper insight into their characters considering at four years old they haven't shown or even discovered their strengths or potentials.

"It's amazing how the palmistry reading told me about the people that my children will become," said their mother. "I always knew that Max was the sensitive one of the two, but it is so lovely to know that Max's sense of responsibility and duty will sustain him and help him form strong relationships. Subsequent to the reading, Max started to develop an interest in drawing and his artistic talent is increasing every day.

"To know that Lucie will be a strong, communicative woman makes me less anxious about her future because as long as we guide her and are sensitive to her manipulative aspects, she will become a woman of substance."

Possible careers for Max

ARCHITECT

INTERIOR DESIGNER

town planner

SET DESIGNER

ceramicist

Possible careers for Lucie

BUSINESSWOMAN

HOSPITALITY INDUSTRY

travel industry

NEGOTIATOR

politician

MAX's hand

Max has a Square palm, which indicates a very organized little person. The raised bumps or "Droplets" on the end of his fingers show a tendency for him to be very tactile and to experience the world very much through his sense of touch. The Writer's Fork in his hand shows strong creative talents. This may be through the use of words or some other form of creativity or self expression such as art. The fat base phalange on each finger is a good sign of a person who appreciates the beauty of life.

Max has a strong sense of duty, indicated by the line to his Saturn finger. He is a responsible character who is likely to have stable relationships. He has a very healthy Life line and is a balanced person.

He has short fingers in relation to his hand, indicating that he is a quick thinker. His high mount of Luna shows that he is very intuitive and will develop a great connection with his unconscious self. It also indicates a great imagination.

Max also has a good and well-formed line of Intuition and the Mystic Cross between his Head and Heart lines, reveals an interest in things relating to the mystical or ethereal aspects of life. He holds his Mercury finger away from the other fingers, this shows that he needs to have his own space. This doesn't mean that he is a loner, only that he needs time to be alone. His Jupiter finger, held apart from the other fingers, means he likes to do his own thing, be independent of others and not follow the crowd.

Max has a strong sense of duty, indicated by the line to Saturn finger. He is a responsible character who is likely to have stable relationships. He has a very healthy Life line and is a balanced person and will show great ambition in his 30s and 40s, as shown by off-shoots from his Life line at those times in his life.

The "waisted" thumb in Max's hand shows conscientiousness and a desire for perfection, not a bad thing if Max should decide to become and architect or town planner!

He also has a nice Apollo line, which should ensure a good amount of success in his life.

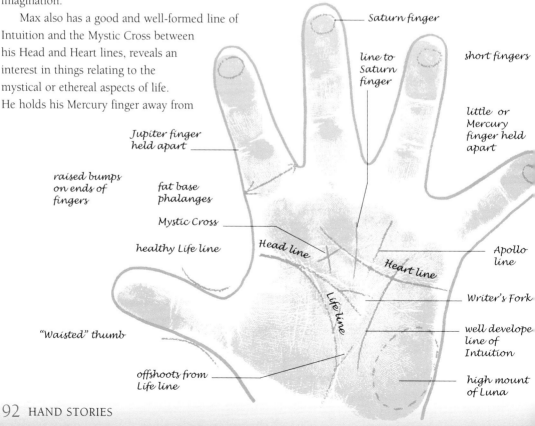

Saturn finger

line to Saturn finger

short fingers

little or Mercury finger held apart

Jupiter finger held apart

raised bumps on ends of fingers

fat base phalanges

Mystic Cross

healthy Life line

Head line

Heart line

Apollo line

Life line

Writer's Fork

"Waisted" thumb

well developed line of Intuition

offshoots from Life line

high mount of Luna

LUCIE's hand

Lucie has quite a long rectangular palm, showing a thoughtful personality. She held her hands out to be read with her fingers showing wide spaces between them ("open handed"), indicating a gregarious and open character. She is someone who has the ability to have a great affinity with many people. Lucie has short fingers and despite her long palm, this shows that she is quick and alert and doesn't miss much. She would be wonderful in the hospitality industry or any kind of work where she was meeting people.

Lucie's Heart line goes right across to the edge of her palm towards her Jupiter finger, which indicates that she is ambitious and may be inclined to allow her ambition to overrule her hearts decisions. Lucie's Life line is broken, which means that she is very likely to change her direction in life. She may do that several times, as there are a few breaks in the line, showing not crises, but life changes.

Lucie's Head line, which is very separate from the Heart line, indicates that she will not be a romantic pushover as she will live her life according to her head and not her heart. Using her mental strength in a career should make her very successful.

Lucie also has a strong line of Intuition, and a well-developed mount of Luna. Her high mounts of Luna and Venus show that she can turn on the charm when she needs to. She can be very manipulative, as shown by her strong thumb and long, strong Jupiter finger and her ambition will enable her to manipulate situations to get the result she wants.

The ring around the base phalange of her thumb shows that she can be very loyal to those whom she admires and loves.

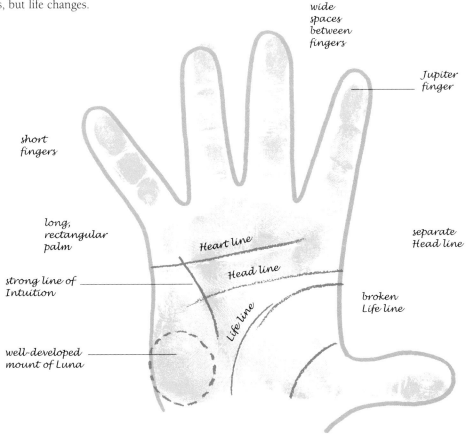

wide spaces between fingers

Jupiter finger

short fingers

long, rectangular palm

strong line of Intuition

well-developed mount of Luna

Heart line

Head line

Life line

separate Head line

broken Life line

Index

Bibliography
A Guide to Modern Palmistry, Beryl Hutchinson, Sphere Books, UK, 1967.
The Art of Hand Analysis, Mir Bashir, Ashgrove Publishing, UK, 1998.
You and Your Hand, Cheiro, Sphere Books, UK, 1977.
Mind Map, Anthony Masters, Eyre Methuen, UK, 1980.
The Benham Book of Palmistry, William. G. Benham, New Page Books, US, 1993.

Acknowledgments
The author would like to thank Paula Le Flohic for her inspiration and help in the early stages of the book's development. Thanks also to my wonderful editor, Amy Carroll, for her insight and her uncanny ability to remind me of the bits I forgot to put in; and to Denise Brown for her wonderful illustrations and her natural grasp of the nuances of hand reading. And, of course, thanks to the delightful children whose hands are appraised in this book.

Carroll and Brown would like to thank:
Production Director Karol Davies
IT Management Paul Stradling
Picture Researcher Sandra Schneider

Picture credits
Front jacket, and pages 30-31, 47 (top left) and 66 courtesy of Photolibrary.